WWW.S

CROWOOD METALWORKING GUIDES

# METAL TURNING
# ON THE LATHE

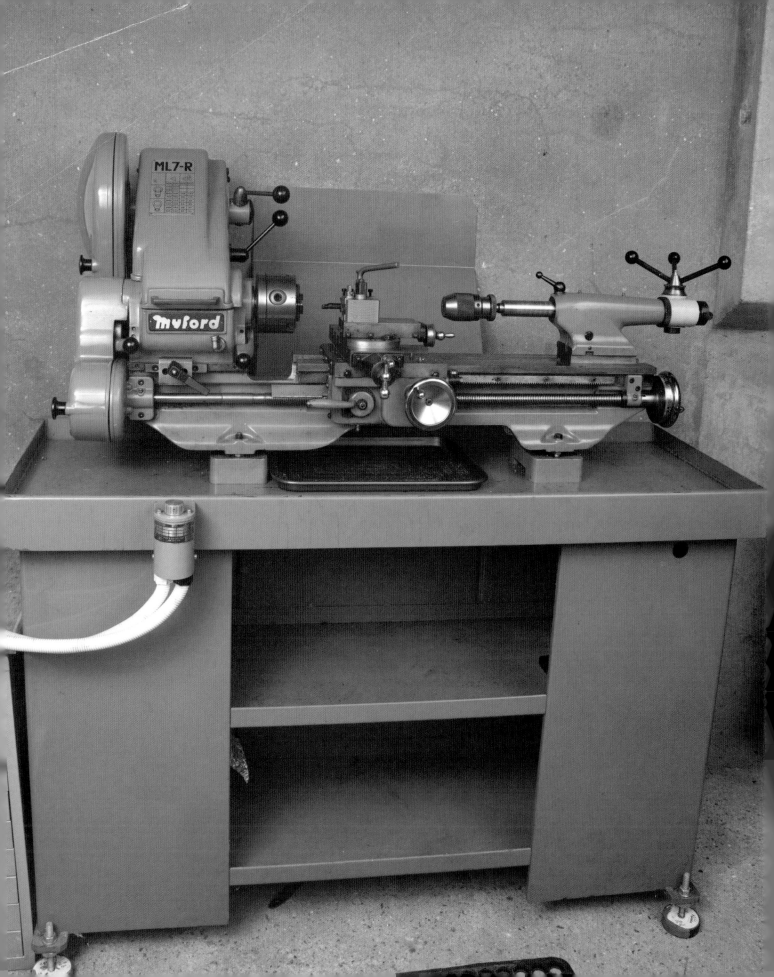

CROWOOD METALWORKING GUIDES

# METAL TURNING ON THE LATHE

**DAVID A. CLARK**

THE CROWOOD PRESS

First published in 2013 by
The Crowood Press Ltd
Ramsbury, Marlborough
Wiltshire SN8 2HR

**www.crowood.com**

**British Library Cataloguing-in-Publication Data**
A catalogue record for this book is available from the British Library.

ISBN 978 1 84797 523 2

Typeset by Jean Cussons Typesetting, Diss, Norfolk
Printed and bound in Malaysia by Times Offset (M) Sdn Bhd

# Contents

# Introduction

The lathe is often called the King of machine tools. It is very versatile and can be used to make all sorts of engineering components. Henry Maudslay, who made his first screwcutting and metal-working lathe in England shortly before 1800, was one of the first engineers to incorporate the slide rest, a leadscrew and change gears into one machine. This made it possible to make interchangeable screw threads, which, in turn, revolutionized the production of machines and machine tools.

This book is for you, the practising or aspiring engineer. Whether you are working in an industrial environment or a home workshop, this book will help you to acquire important new skills and give you insider tips you won't find elsewhere.

Perhaps you don't have a knowledgeable friend to teach you or you aren't able to join a club. It does not matter what previous experience you have, this book will teach you the basics of lathe work from first principles to advanced turning techniques. You will find all you need to know within these pages.

During more than thirty years in the engineering industry I have worked with many engineers, both beginners and experts, and have taught many young people during their first steps into engineering. Working as a self-employed engineer, I learnt quick and accurate ways of working, both from my own experience and from other engineers. Since 2008 I have edited *Model Engineer* and *Model Engineers' Workshop*, the two main UK magazines for machining in the home workshop, and this has given me an insight into what amateur (and sometimes professional) engineers are looking for. I have also been able to advise many amateur engineers on how to solve their workshop problems or just to get them started on the right lines.

*Model Engineer, which currently appears every fortnight, has been published continuously since 1898. It is mainly about making precision models but often includes techniques for turning in the lathe.*

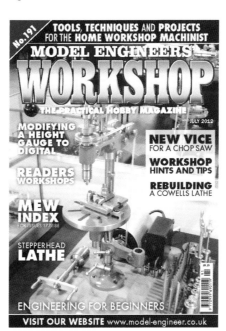

*Model Engineers' Workshop, introduced in 1990, is a relative newcomer to the model engineering scene. It deals mainly with tools and processes and is now published every four weeks.*

I would like to pass on some of this knowledge. This book, *Metal Turning on the Lathe*, is the first of three for Crowood Press on aspects of workshop engineering; it will be followed by *Milling* and *Introduction to Workshop Tools and Techniques*. Each book will be a comprehensive guide for both the amateur and professional engineer.

A lathe is essential to all but the most basic of workshops. It enables you to produce turned components to a high degree of accuracy with the minimum of effort.

*OPPOSITE: A Myford lathe dating from the mid-twentieth century, as supplied to Gamages, a London department store.*

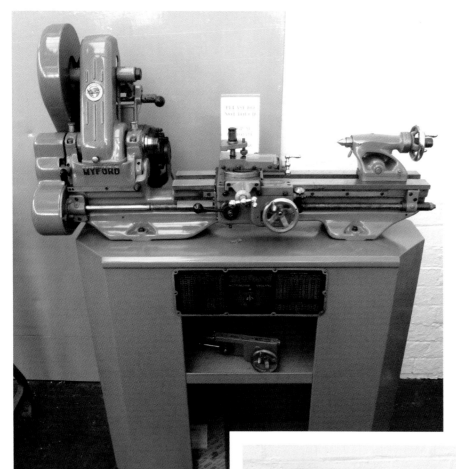

The basic Myford model, the ML7, was manufactured for many years. Tens of thousands are still to be found in garages, factories and home workshops around the world. This is the prototype ML7 Lathe as rebuilt by Myford Ltd.

The later ML7R and Super 7 models were fitted with a clutch as standard. This saves wear and tear on the electrical components and the motor. They also had more speeds. Later versions of the Super 7 can be found with a power cross feed. The illustration shows the prototype Super 7 lathe; again it has been rebuilt to factory standards by Myford Ltd.

The A to Z of a lathe: (A) Change wheel guard; (B) Countershaft pulley guard; (C) Drive belt guard; (D) Countershaft; (E) Belt tension lever; (F) Oiler; (G) Motor; (H) Tumbler gear operating lever; (I) Headstock; (J) Back gear operating lever; (K) Mandrel nose; (L) Left-hand leadscrew bearing; (M) Leadscrew; (N) Half nut operating lever; (O) Tool clamp; (P) Top slide; (Q) Cross slide; (R) Saddle; (S) Apron; (T) Carriage handwheel; (U) Screw thread indicator; (V) Lathe bed; (W) Rack; (X) Tailstock; (Y) Tailstock handwheel; (Z) Right-hand leadscrew bearing.

An early Myford lathe. Although very basic, it can do a lot of useful work in the workshop, especially if time is spent on making a few simple accessories.

This book will show you how to use the lathe safely and effectively in your workshop, but first you should ensure that you are familiar with the main parts of the lathe and their terminology, which may be found on page 9.

Chapter 1 of this book is about choosing a lathe, what size of lathe to buy, the different types available, desirable features, and whether you should buy new or second-hand.

Chapter 2 covers installing a lathe, how to lubricate it and maintain it in good condition, and advice on general safety in your workshop with particular emphasis on how to use a lathe safely.

Chapter 3 will look at the materials from which cutting tools are made, as well as their basic shape and geometry. Then we will look at selecting suitable speeds and feeds.

Chapter 4 deals with sharpening lathe tools and how to set them up in the lathe.

Chapter 5 covers the different types of chucks, how to use them and set work up accurately in them.

Chapter 6 teaches you basic turning between centres and then introduces turning with the work mounted on the lathe faceplate.

Chapter 7 is about holding work in a collet, and how you can make and use several different types of mandrel for workholding.

Chapter 8 explains how to turn a taper using the top slide, the use of fixed and travelling steadies and making a form tool.

Chapter 9 explains how to use drills and reamers in the lathe, including how to select the correct speeds and feeds.

Chapter 10 shows the different ways to bore holes in the lathe: with the work held in a chuck, mounted on the faceplate or held on the cross slide.

Chapter 11 explains how to use knurling tools and radius turning tools, as well as making simple form tools and basic production methods.

Chapter 12 shows you how to use taps and dies to cut internal and external threads in the lathe. It also explains how to set up a simple gear train and cut a screw thread with the help of a screwcutting dial indicator.

# 1   *Buying Your First Lathe*

## WHAT SIZE OF LATHE DO I REQUIRE?

The first thing to consider when buying a lathe is the size of the work that you want to do. What is the largest diameter you will want to turn on it and what is the longest length you will need to turn? A 3½ × 18in (90 × 457mm) lathe will allow a maximum diameter of 7in (178mm) to be turned over the lathe bed; the latter figure is known as the swing. In practice, though, this is a theoretical maximum as it is still necessary to hold and clamp the article being turned. The swing over the cross slide is usually much smaller, typically 2in (50mm).

Many lathes, however, are manufactured with a gap bed at the headstock end to enable short items of a large diameter, such as locomotive or traction engine wheels, to be turned.

Lathes are also sometimes available as standard and long bed lathes. The long bed lathe, as the name suggests, allows longer material to be turned within the capacity of the lathe. When turning longer material, the diameter will be limited by the swing over the cross slide. This will be a lot smaller than the swing over the bed.

If building a model such as a traction engine or a locomotive, the deciding factor for the size of lathe is likely to be the diameter of the largest pair of wheels that need to be turned. Before deciding on the size of lathe required you should determine the size of the largest diameter and the longest length of material that needs to be turned. Another factor in determining what

lathe to buy is the availability of spares and accessories: is the company still trading, will it still be trading in the future, and are there large amounts of second-hand parts and accessories available from tool dealers or on eBay?

## LATHE ELECTRICS

Single phase electric is where the lathe plugs into the mains supply in your house. The motor will have the usual live, neutral and earth leads. Lathes supplied for factory use usually have three phase motors and require three live wires, each of a different phase. Think of a phase as an incoming wave on the seashore; three successive waves make up the three phases needed. Each phase is the same as the preceding one but they are out of sync and all peak at a different time.

### Converters and inverters

You can run some 3 phase motors from a single phase supply via a converter or an inverter. The motor information plate will usually say 240 volts/440 volts if it is capable of running on an inverter. Inside the motor there will be changeover tags to change the

*A typical inverter to convert 240 volts single phase to 240 volts 3 phase.*

*A forward/reverse control box for an inverter.*

motor from 440V down to 240V. Follow the converter/inverter manufacturer's instructions for further information. It is not usually very complicated to run a 240V 3 phase motor from an inverter and this will give a quieter and smoother running motor than a single phase supply can provide. This usually requires some simple programming, explained in the inverter's instructions, and it usually takes five minutes to get the motor working properly.

The inverter runs at a constant voltage but the speed of the motor will change as the frequency is raised or lowered. I suggest limiting your inverter from full speed to half speed so that the fan still cools the motor and stops it from overheating; you can then use the belts to change the main speed steps as usual. (If you must use very slow running it is possible to add a separate fan, such as a computer cooling fan, to give constant airflow.) Most inverter suppliers offer a forward/reverse and speed control box that can be set up in a convenient position on the machine. These are well worth fitting for convenience in use.

While inverters are designed to run only

*This motor is part of the inverter package shown in the previous illustration. No wiring is involved as the motor lead plugs straight into the inverter box.*

one machine, you can get converters to power more than one machine at a time. Depending on the size and power output, converters cost about three to four times as much as an inverter.

There are two main types of converter. Rotary converters are designed to run more than one motor at a time. This is ideal if you want to run more than one machine or two motors on one machine, for example the main machine motor and perhaps an auxiliary motor that drives the machine's coolant pump or power feed system.

*A rotary converter capable of powering more than one 3 phase motor.*

The second type is the static converter, which is designed to run one motor at a time. There is, of course, nothing to stop you using the static converter on more than one machine by fitting a suitable female electrical connector to the static converter and matching male connectors to the individual machines. This way you can connect the static converter to only one machine at a time.

*This inverter is designed for mounting on the front of the lathe.*

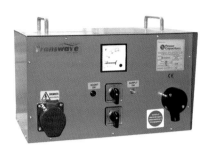

*This static converter is suitable for powering one 3 phase motor. If you fit a socket on the output, however, different individual machines can be plugged into it, one at a time.*

The electrical loading on rotary or static converters must not exceed their maximum rating. If in doubt on the load capacity needed to run your machine(s), you should consult the manufacturer or supplier of the converter.

### Simple electrical testing and safety

When buying a small single phase second-hand lathe, take with you an earth leakage tester of the type used for lawn mowers and other garden tools. I once bought a Unimat 3 lathe, took it home and plugged it in. It kept blowing the earth leakage trip in the fuse box, even though it had worked perfectly at the seller's house. I sold it on at a loss but the buyer did know there was a problem with the electrics.

It is most important that the metal parts of any lathe are connected to the earth wire, which is in turn connected to earth. Make sure that the motor frame is also connected to earth as some motors have dampening rubber mounts that insulate them from the machine itself. If in doubt about any aspect of electrical installation, please consult a qualified electrician.

### LATHE BED

The lathe bed is the backbone of the entire lathe and is the part that is mounted on the bench or stand. There are two main types of lathe bed: the plain bed and the gap bed. The plain bed is usually continuous all the way along its length while the gap bed has, as its name suggests, a gap in the bed. This is not a literal gap but a stepped section that allows bigger diameters to be turned than you would otherwise be able to turn on a plain bed lathe. This gap is a means of making a lathe smaller than would be required for a plain lathe able to turn a similar size of component.

Some continuous lathe beds have a section next to the headstock that can be removed to increase the diameter that can be turned. This feature is usually only fitted to larger lathes such as are mostly found in factories.

Some lathes have hardened beds although most are just plain cast iron. There are three main types of bed ways, called shears: the plain flat bed with square ways, a bed with a flat top and a 60 degree dovetail at each side, and a bed with raised and inverted Vee ways. On the last of these the tailstock usually runs on one set of Vees and the carriage on a different set of Vees, resulting in less wear to the main slides. Wide beds are better and more accurate, as

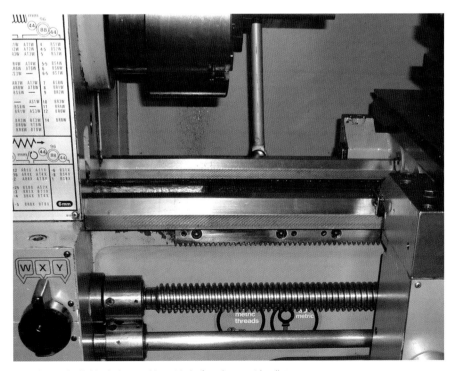

*An earth leakage trip is ideal for quickly eliminating a motor where the electrical insulation is breaking down. It is useful for detecting certain electrical earthing faults but should not be used as a guarantee of electrical safety.*

*A continuous bed is ideal when working with the faceplate or with collets.*

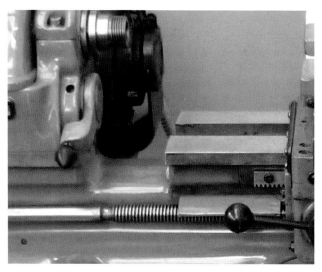

*Close-up view of a typical lathe bed with a gap. A gap bed lathe has a larger turning diameter capacity than the equivalent sized continuous bed lathe.*

years and many second-hand examples are still available. This model differs from most lathes in that it has two steel bars as a bed. This is not a problem, however, as the Unimat is intended only for very small and lightweight model-making work and there is the advantage that the bed can be replaced by fitting new bars.

When buying a second-hand lathe, it is most important to check the condition of the bed. You need to make sure the bed is reasonably free from dings, rust and hacksaw marks. Hacksaw marks near the headstock are often caused by sawing off work while it is held in the chuck; dings are usually caused by dropping the chuck on the lathe bed when screwing it on or off the mandrel.

*The Myford range of lathes has a square form of bed.*

the lathe carriage is less likely to twist on a wide bed.

Some very early lathes, such as those made by Drummond, had a round bed. Although they worked well, there is no adjustment for wear in the lathe bed.

The Unimat SL lathe was sold for many

*A lathe bed with raised and inverted Vees. The carriage usually slides on one set of Vees and the tailstock slides on the other.*

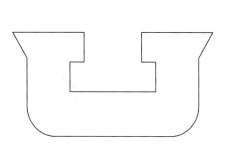

*This type of bed has a flat top with an inverted Vee at each side. The Vees are usually set at 60 degrees but can vary with different makers.*

*A modern Chinese lathe bed with an inverted raised Vee. The carriage and tailstock usually slide on the same Vee.*

A simple chuck board placed on the bed while fitting or removing the chuck will protect the bed. It is also ideal for protecting the bed when filing or hacksawing work in the chuck.

Wear is most commonly found at the headstock end of the lathe as a result of machining many short components and relatively few long ones. Make sure the lathe carriage is properly adjusted at the headstock and then run it along as far as you can towards the tailstock. The carriage should be reasonably free but not loose all the way along the bed.

A flat bed lathe with square bedways, such as a Myford, can be checked for wear on the lathe bed using a micrometer or vernier. Check over the working part of the lathe bed on which the carriage slides rather than the part that is not used for guidance. Check both the width and the thickness of the bed ways.

The tailstock should also be a good

*Old round bed Drummond lathes are still available second-hand. This particular example is treadle driven.*

*The Unimat SL is a very popular small lathe. Its bed consists of two steel bars that can be replaced very easily with silver steel if they get worn or, more likely, when they get rusty.*

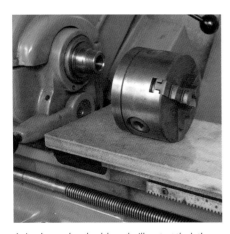

*A simple wooden chuck board will protect the lathe bed from dings and hacksaw marks.*

sliding fit on any guiding surfaces. Wear is most likely to be found on the tenon that slides between the bed ways. A worn tenon could probably be replaced, but there is not much you can do if the tenon guides are worn. The only way to fix a worn bed requires a complete bed regrind. This is likely to be expensive so it would be better to look for an unworn lathe. Decent unworn lathes are out there, since many model engineers may have bought them new forty or fifty years ago and hardly used them.

## LATHE HEADSTOCK

The headstock is the large component mounted at the left-hand side of the lathe bed. It needs to have good bearings. An all-geared head will almost certainly have ball or roller races while the older type of lathe for amateurs may well have plain bearings, either phosphor bronze or white-metal. These are perfectly adequate but you should make sure there is no wear in them. Some lathes also have a mandrel that runs directly in bored holes in the cast iron headstock casting. Plain bearings will be perfectly satisfactory as long as adequate lubrication is used.

To check for wear in the lathe's bearings, fit a chuck to the mandrel and put a dial test

*Close-up view of a Myford headstock on an ML7R. Note the large bronze bearing at the front. The earlier ML7 lathes had white metal bearings, although the C7 capstan had bronze bearings and a hardened lathe spindle.*

*Checking the lathe bearings for wear. Any movement up and down indicates wear in the bearing.*

indicator on top of the chuck. Gently try levering the chuck up and down by using a steel bar or similar held in the chuck. You are looking for minimal movement here, especially on a headstock fitted with ball races.

The mandrel is mounted in the headstock and is usually threaded to take a chuck or faceplate. The lathe's mandrel should not move back and forth in the bearings. If it does, however, it will probably be possible to adjust it to correct any endwise movement. The mandrel should not be too stiff but should turn easily by hand.

When testing a lathe, make sure the headstock bearings are correctly adjusted so that, where possible, there is no play. Set a tool up, take a trial cut along a length of bar and check for chatter. If you are using a correctly set tool and a suitable speed, chatter is a sure sign of worn bearings.

## POWER DRIVE

*Many lathes have a three- or four-step drive pulley as the second stage of the drive chain.*

Many lathes have a three- or four-step pulley on the mandrel to take the drive from a similar pulley on the countershaft. The coun-

*This particular lathe has a two-step motor pulley and countershaft, which doubles the available speeds.*

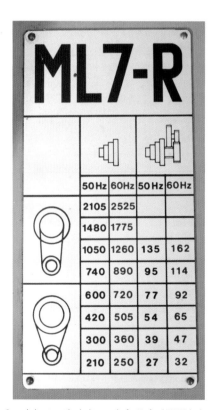

*Speed chart on the belt guard of a Myford ML7R lathe.*

*The clutch is normally mounted inside the large countershaft pulley. It is usually operated by a lever at the right-hand side of the headstock, attached to a push rod that passes right through the countershaft.*

tershaft is in turn driven from the motor, which is often mounted at the back of the headstock and completes the integral drive system that is so popular on most amateurs' lathes.

A few lathes have a clutch fitted as standard or as an optional extra. The clutch saves having to start and stop the motor while it is running. This helps to stop wear and tear on the motor and electrical system.

A different type of clutch system, the TriLeva speed selector, was only fitted to Myford ML7 or C7 lathes. This has three levers for setting three different speeds. Depending on the lever you depress, you get a high, medium or low speed. If you press one of the levers down while another is right down, the first lever will disengage

the second, so stopping the mandrel from going round. If the lathe is switched off and all three handles are depressed, the mandrel is locked, preventing rotation. This is useful if filing or hacksawing in the lathe.

*The Myford TriLeva attachment will only fit ML7 and C7 lathes and is not suitable for ML7R or Super 7 lathes.*

There has been a trend in recent years to do away with the countershaft and pulley system and to replace the motor with a variable speed one with an electronic controller. This is acceptable, except that at low revolutions it does not provide the torque that can be obtained from a countershaft system. There is also the disadvantage that there is no way to drive the lathe if the controller circuit board fails, whereas you can just fit a new one if the belt breaks. The board could, of course, be fixed provided that a circuit diagram is available and the electronic components can be identified. Sometimes the components are marked with internal house numbers rather than commercially recognized part numbers that can be ordered as a replacement from a catalogue. Some boards might even have the identification marks removed to make repairs almost impossible.

*The threaded end of a lathe mandrel is designed so that the chuck backplate runs true. If the chuck mounting face of the backplate is machined in situ, the chuck should run true as well.*

## CHUCK MOUNTING SYSTEMS

The threaded lathe mandrel nose is not, by itself, a suitable location for a chuck or faceplate so the nose is usually given a turned register on which to locate the chuck. The chuck is screwed right onto the mandrel, over the register, and butts up to a turned collar to keep the chuck running true. The other side of the mandrel collar butts up against the main headstock bearing, which usually acts as a thrust face.

The mandrel is usually bored through and machined to take a Morse taper centre for turning between centres. Do not put your finger in either end of the mandrel to clean it while the lathe is running. An easy way to clean the taper in the headstock is with a bottle brush, often sold in chemists to clean babies' bottles. An alternative is a soft felt shotgun brush; do not use one made from wire.

There are various systems of chuck mounting in use, especially on the larger lathes. The problem with the screw-on type with a register, mentioned above, is that the chuck or faceplate can unscrew when the lathe is running in reverse. The only time you should run this type of mandrel in reverse, very slowly and without taking a cut, is if you need to return the screwcutting tool to the start of the thread you are cutting.

Alternative spindle noses can be a plain

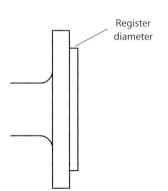

*This lathe has a plain register. Accuracy relies on the lathe chuck being a good fit on the register.*

Register diameter

*An American standard Cam Lock chuck mounting backplate and Cam Lock chuck plate fitted to a chuck. They are usually fitted to larger industrial lathes.*

disc with a register to bolt the chuck on to, or a cam lock where the chuck is held on tightly by turning studs to lock the chuck onto the mandrel. The plain disc with register relies on having chucks with a mating register to work properly.

The American D style Cam Lock system

*The leadscrew is driven from the mandrel via a gear train.*

mounted on a lever at the left of the head-stock. The direction of the leadscrew can be changed by bringing either one or the other into gear by raising or lowering a lever. There is usually a central neutral position where neither gear is in mesh. This saves wear on the lathe changewheels and leadscrew bearings as well as reducing noise while working. Mandrel and tumbler gears will be discussed further in Chapter 12 when we set up a screwcutting gear train.

A set of changewheels usually comprises about a dozen gears, but this can vary depending on the manufacturer. These changewheels, which take the drive from the tumbler gears down to the leadscrew, are mounted on moveable studs to ensure the gears are in mesh with each other. Depending on the number of gears in the train, the leadscrew will turn either clockwise or anti-clockwise. The direction of the leadscrew can be reversed using the tumbler gears to enable right-hand or left-hand threads to be cut.

You can usually set the gears to cut a very fine pitch so that the leadscrew acts as a self feed when turning from the saddle. If you anticipate the need to do any screwcutting,

either takes a chuck or faceplate directly or it has a backplate that can have a register turned on it to suit the required chuck. Although many lathe mandrels with Cam Lock fittings have six holes, the matching chuck or faceplate often has only three locking pins.

The advantage of both of the last two systems is that they can be run in reverse without the chuck coming off the mandrel.

## SCREWCUTTING GEARS

The left-hand end of the mandrel will often have a gear mounted on it to drive the changewheel gears and leadscrew.

The mandrel gear usually drives a pair of gears called tumbler gears, which are

*Often there are tumbler gears in the gear train that can reverse the direction of the leadscrew.*

*Make sure that a full set of change gears is included with the lathe. If not, they are readily available second-hand.*

*This lathe has both a leadscrew for screwcutting and a drive shaft for the saddle and cross slide feeds.*

check that the supplied screwcutting gears will do the range of pitches you require. It has been known for certain lathes to be unable to handle some common pitches, a typical example being 26 TPI (teeth per inch). A pitch of 26 TPI is often needed to repair motorcycles and bikes made before the introduction of metrication.

## LEADSCREW

The leadscrew is mounted at the front of the lathe; there are usually bearings to sup-

*Most leadscrews can have a graduated handwheel mounted on the right-hand end of the leadscrew.*

port the leadscrew at either end of the lathe bed. It is used to move the lathe saddle along the bed, either for a self acting feed or for screwcutting. Some lathes also have a graduated handwheel mounted at the right-hand end of the leadscrew for turning the mandrel by hand.

Some of the larger lathes also have a separate feed shaft, which is usually a plain round shaft with a keyway cut along it to drive the saddle using a fine feed. This saves wear and tear on the leadscrew, which is then only used for screwcutting.

## SCREWCUTTING FACILITIES

A useful feature on any lathe is the ability to cut screw threads of different pitches. Lead-screws come in different pitches, a common one being 8 TPI, but many variations are fitted to different lathes including leadscrews

with a metric pitch. It is awkward to machine metric screws with an imperial leadscrew and vice versa. Sometimes metric conversion sets are available but they can be hard to find, are usually expensive and require the lathe to be changed over, often using 127 tooth gear wheels. This figure is derived from multiplying the metric equivalent of 1in (25.4mm) by five; a 127 tooth wheel is thus a direct conversion to a metric thread on a lathe with an imperial leadscrew. A 127 tooth gear is usually very large if it matches the pitch of the remaining screwcutting gears, but you could use smaller gears with a smaller DP (diametral pitch) but still with 127 teeth. You would also need a matching gear of, say, fifty teeth to give you a 2.54:1 ratio.

A screwcutting dial indicator, usually mounted to the right of the carriage, is a useful feature. This is a small dial, with divisions marked on it, mounted on a shaft. The other end of the shaft has a gear that meshes with the leadscrew and makes the dial go round. When the clasp nuts are engaged the carriage moves and, as the gear moves

*A typical screw thread dial indicator. This one is engaged and disengaged by loosening the bolt and engaging the drive gear with the leadscrew.*

depends on the pitch of the thread being cut. Some thread pitches allow you to engage at any division of the dial while others need to be engaged at a particular position of the dial. The use of the screwcutting dial indicator will be covered in Chapter 12. When using the fine feed, you can engage the clasp nuts at any marked position on the dial, so avoiding wear to the clasp nuts.

## LATHE SADDLE AND APRON

The saddle is the part that slides on top of the lathe bed and usually has the cross slide and top slide mounted on it. The apron is mounted to the front of the saddle. You should make sure there is no play in the saddle, either sideways or up and down, and that it travels freely from one end of the lathe bed to the other with no tight spots. At the front, nearest the operator, there is usually a pair of clasp nuts (these are split nuts). These can be engaged or disengaged from the leadscrew for screwcutting or moving the saddle along with the leadscrew. On cheaper lathes there is usually a solid nut that cannot be disengaged.

There is often a rack at the front of the

lathe bed that matches up with a handle and gears on the lathe apron. This can be used to move the carriage along the bed without wearing out the leadscrew. Some lathes have the carriage feed wheel on the right but others have it on the left, where hot swarf can fall onto your hands. The cheaper lathes have no rack and rely on the leadscrew to wind the carriage back and forth.

## CROSS SLIDE

On top of the carriage is the cross slide, which can be wound back and forth across the lathe bed. When using the cross slide for facing across the work, the carriage should be locked to stop it moving along the bed. Lathes for amateur use are more likely to have a Tee-slotted cross slide, while larger commercial lathes are unlikely to have this facility. The Tee-slotted cross slide is very useful, especially if you don't have a milling machine. You can bolt work to the cross slide for machining using a cutter in the chuck or for boring workpieces that are too large to swing in the chuck.

at the same speed as the carriage, the dial stops going round.

When you engage the clasp nuts on the leadscrew, the position where you engage

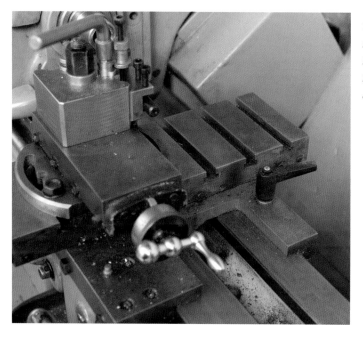

*The lathe saddle slides along the lathe bed. The apron is bolted to the front of the saddle.*

*A Tee-slotted cross slide makes the small lathe more versatile.*

Zero setting dials are desirable for both the cross slide and the topslide. They allow you to set the dial to zero, which makes it easier to measure the amount you are taking off with one cut. In use, wind the tool up

*Zero setting dials make turning and screwcutting to depth very easy.*

*A pair of zero setting dials ready to fit.*

## TOP SLIDE

The top slide is mounted on top of the cross slide. The top slide is normally set at 90 degrees to the cross slide, although it can usually be swivelled around to various angles for turning a taper, an angle, or for screwcutting. Some of the cheaper lathes don't have a top slide as standard but it is a very useful feature if you can get one. The top slide should be able to rotate, especially for screwcutting, but the top slide handle may foul the cross slide in certain positions, so check if this is a problem. The turning tool is usually mounted on the top of the top slide. It can either be clamped on directly, usually with packing strips underneath, or the tool can be mounted in a tool holder such as a three- or four-way tool post or a quick-change tool post. We will look at tool holding methods in Chapter 4 when discussing setting up turning tools.

## TAILSTOCK

The component at the right-hand end of the lathe is the tailstock. This usually has a hand-

power cross feed for facing. This does not matter as you can easily wind the cross slide across by hand. The only time I have found a power cross feed to be of use is when I had to face across a faceplate to true it up. I have trued up similar size faceplates by hand; it just took a little longer.

*The top slide is mounted on the cross slide.*

to the work and touch on, set the dial to zero and wind the tool back off from the work. You now know where zero is on the tool and can take the required depth of cut without having to work it out.

Lathes can be purchased with imperial or metric feed screws. Most model designs are imperial, but metric is making headway and this may well be the way to go. Beware lathes with imperial feed screws and metric dials. Typically these will have a funny number of handwheel divisions rather than a whole number. Most of the lathes you might come across are unlikely to have a

*A lathe tailstock with the barrel extended. Note that it is not usually a problem if the chuck key is left in the tailstock while not in use.*

ing to a particular hole depth are very useful but are not often included on the cheaper lathes, although industrial lathes usually have graduated tailstock handwheels. The better makes of lathe have a lever clamping tailstock arrangement, while the cheaper lathes often have a clamping spanner or an Allen screw clamp.

## MACHINE GUARDS

The drive motor, countershaft (if fitted) and pulley belts should all be properly guarded. It is very easy to get caught up in an unguarded machine and the consequences can be quite nasty. This has never happened to me, but I have seen someone caught up in a machine and it was not very nice. I do recommend that you make sure your machine guards are correctly fitted.

wheel to feed a drill into the work, but lever-feed and capstan-style feeding mechanisms are also available. You can lock the tailstock anywhere along the bed. The tailstock has a barrel inside it that can be wound in and out to give a linear movement to drill a hole in work held in the chuck. The tailstock is usually bored to a Morse taper, often of a similar size to the headstock, so it can take accessories such as drill chucks mounted on a Morse taper. It can also take a centre for turning work between centres. It is important that both the headstock and tailstock tapers are free from marks, scratches and burrs.

Adjustment is usually provided between the base and the main body of the tailstock to allow for setting the tailstock in line with the headstock. Tailstocks can be self ejecting, where the tool is extracted as it is wound back, while some tailstocks have a through hole and need a tap with a bar to remove the tool. Handwheel depth graduations for drill-

*All guards should be fitted in place before operating the lathe.*

## OTHER DESIRABLE FEATURES

Digital readouts are useful on a lathe as they can show you how much to move the handwheels and how much material has been taken off. They are quite expensive but you can fit them yourself if you are careful. Unfortunately, most of the cheaper versions dislike soluble oil or other coolant if you get it into the readout head.

*The Myford 'Norton' style quick-change screwcutting gearbox.*

*A digital readout suitable for mounting on a lathe.*

*Soluble oil pumps and reservoirs are readily obtainable.*

average second-hand lathe. A Myford Norton gearbox has twenty-four pitches and is controlled by two levers. Reversing two gears in the Myford changewheel train gives

*The cone gears inside a typical Norton screwcutting gearbox (not an original Myford one).*

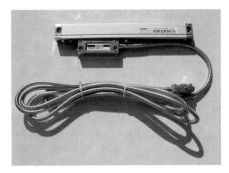

*You will need two slides, one for each axis.*

A soluble pump for cutting fluid is useful and often comes fitted as standard on the larger lathes. However, a tin of cutting oil and a brush will be good enough for most work and that may suit you fine.

A Norton quick-change screwcutting gearbox saves time as you don't have to set up changewheel trains. A gearbox, however, considerably increases the price of the

*For most jobs, you can get away with some cutting oil, a bowl and a brush.*

the gearbox twenty-four fine feeds instead of the twenty-four screwcutting pitches. The gearbox has a set of gears arranged as a cone. By sliding the lever along and dropping the master gear onto the cone, you can change the gearbox ratio and so the pitch.

*Several designs have been published to make your own Norton type screwcutting gearbox. This one is available from Hemingway Kits.*

can be switched in or out to reduce the speed of the lathe by a ratio of usually about 5:1, depending on the maker, to enable you to turn large diameter workpieces. This reduction is also essential on a screwcutting lathe as otherwise the mandrel will be going too fast while screwcutting and you won't be able to stop in the right place at the end of the thread.

If buying a back-geared lathe, check that both gear wheels have all their teeth. It is a major job to strip down a lathe and fit new gear wheels, assuming they are even available as spares.

Check the lathe in all gear ranges with the lathe running. If a back-geared lathe or an all-geared head is noisy, it could indicate wear; it will also be a nuisance in your workshop, as no one wants to hear a noisy machine running. Noise could be a major problem, especially if you have neighbours nearby.

Geared heads usually have a wide range of speeds: the larger industrial lathes can go up to speeds of 2,000rpm and smaller versions are often higher.

## SPINDLE SPEEDS

The speed range needed on a lathe depends on the work it is required to do. A good range of spindle speeds is desirable with no obvious gaps. With electronic control, this should not be too much of a problem.

Ideally a back-geared lathe would be best but this means either a good second-hand machine, such as a Myford or a Boxford, or alternatively one of the larger Asian-made lathes with an all-geared headstock.

Back gear normally consists of four gears, two large ones and two small ones, which

*This back gear arrangement is switched in and out by turning the toggle on the pulley and lifting a lever at the front of the lathe.*

*An all-geared head on a modern industrial size lathe.*

On the more usual amateurs' lathe there is often a countershaft, usually tensioned by a lever, which tightens up the belt ready for use. The middle speed of the countershaft is usually chosen to be about one quarter of the motor speed. Most small lathes have three speeds and the back gear arrangement adds another three speeds, giving six in all. The Myford Super 7 range of lathes have four speeds and back gear, making eight speeds, but there is also a double pulley on the motor countershaft section, making sixteen speeds in all, although the very lowest back-geared speeds will rarely, if ever, be used.

Some of the older Colchester Chipmaster lathes have what is known as a Kopp Variator drive. This is a variable speed drive controlled by a dial and the system works well, but the Variator is very hard to replace if the drive fails.

This small Cowells lathe is capable of decent work and at the time of writing is probably the only lathe still being made in Britain.

## MOUNTING THE LATHE

There are three main options for mounting a lathe: bench mounting, portable or on a stand. Ideally, a maker's stand should be used for mounting a medium to large lathe, and the stand is often an integral part of larger lathes. A smaller lathe, such as a Unimat or a Cowell, can be mounted on a wooden chopping board or a similar small board. These lathes can be put away in a cupboard after use.

The alternative is a workbench but these are often made from wood, which can expand or contract depending on the moisture in the air. Wood is not a good material from which to make a stand for a larger lathe as it will attract moisture and may expand, shrink or distort. A metal stand is a better option. We will look at installing the lathe in Chapter 2.

An Arc Euro Trade C3 screwcutting lathe made by Sieg. This is a very popular entry level lathe and many accessories are available.

*A medium-sized screwcutting lathe suitable for garden shed workshops.*

The main thing to consider, though, is the attitude of the supplier. Were they willing to talk to you and answer your questions, either at an exhibition or over the phone? How long do they take to answer the phone when you ring their service department? Do they know the answer to a simple question straight away or do they have to get back to you? Is the manual written in English or Chinglish (translated awkwardly from Mandarin or Cantonese)?

There are several suppliers of new lathes in most countries around the world, but the majority of lathes are made in the Far East. Often supplier A's machines come from the same factory as supplier B's: they are just painted a different colour and have different names and labels fitted.

Aftersales service can vary greatly. Usually companies that have been in business longer will offer better aftersales service, but other people's experiences can be found on Internet forums or at local model engineering clubs.

## SHOULD I BUY NEW OR SECOND-HAND?

Beginners setting up a workshop often ask if it is better to buy a new lathe or second-hand. The preceding pages should have given some guidance, but there are more points to be taken into consideration.

### Buying New

The list of lathe suppliers included at the back of this book were all in business at the time of writing. Most will be willing to demonstrate their range of machines at their premises or while attending model engineering exhibitions. Pay close attention to mechanical noise, the general paint finish and the working slideway surfaces, which should be ground. Does the machine have sharp or rough edges? (Handwheels are especially prone to sharp edges.)

*A larger industrial lathe with a foot-operated emergency cut-off switch and brake.*

Usually the Asian lathes are reasonably well made but they often suffer from having plastic gears instead of metal ones. One or two companies supply metal gears as standard, so it is worth asking if their machines have metal or plastic drive gears. Some companies also offer after-market replacement metal gears.

## Buying Second-hand

There are many good quality second-hand machines available, but there is also a lot of worn-out rubbish. If possible, take a knowledgeable friend with you when purchasing a lathe. Be careful when buying at online auctions such as eBay. Most sellers are genuine but some are not. Never part with the cash until you have checked the lathe over. I have bought on eBay without problems but I am careful what I buy and who from. A small lathe for a couple of hundred pounds is unlikely to break the bank if it is a bit of a dog, but a lathe that costs several hundred pounds is a different matter. The green Myford ML7R pictured throughout this book was purchased from eBay. It was brand new, the motor had never been fitted and it was a bargain when compared with the retail price. I did pay cash on collection, but I would have walked away if it had not matched the description in any way.

Whether purchasing new or second-hand, check what accessories come as part of the package and what will need to be purchased separately. Essential tooling can often double the cost of a new machine if it is not included in the price, while dedicated tooling may not even be available for a second-hand bargain lathe.

You should now have an idea of the size of lathe you need, the function of the different parts of the lathe and whether you are buying new or second-hand. In Chapter 2 we will look at installing the lathe and safety in the workshop.

# 2 Installing the Lathe and Using It Safely

If you are buying a new lathe, complete with delivery to your workshop, you can go straight to the section on setting the lathe up. If you are collecting the lathe yourself, however, you should pay attention to a few words on moving it.

## MOVING THE LATHE

When going to collect your lathe, make sure someone will be there to help you load it or take someone with you. Unless it is a miniature lathe, it will be too heavy for one person to lift. Help is also needed when you get the lathe home. Lifting the lathe out of a car can be harder than lifting it in. It is advisable to have three people when unloading: two

at the heavy headstock end and one lifting the lighter tailstock end. You can rent or buy an engine hoist for a reasonable price and this can make moving the machine easier.

If the machine is a substantial industrial type, it would be best to hire a transport company that specializes in machinery removals. Professional machinery removers will usually have properly equipped transport to move heavy machines. This will probably work out cheaper than attempting to do it yourself, but make sure they have insurance in place in case they damage the lathe or your property. You should also ensure they know it has to be put in place as required in the workshop; you don't want half a ton of machinery

dumped on your drive with no way of moving it into position.

Lathes are usually top heavy when being moved and can tip over if you are not careful. The Myford ML7 series, for example, often has the motor and countershaft bolted to the back of the lathe bed and this type of lathe will tend to tip backwards. A simple solution is to bolt two lengths of wood, about 4 × 2in (100 × 50mm), to the lathe feet. One bolt in each end will do if you can't drill holes in the correct position. This will stop the lathe tipping backwards and also make it easier to lift. If possible you should remove the tailstock. This is often a heavy lump of metal but it is usually very easy to slide it off the end of the lathe bed.

*If you have room to manoeuvre, an engine hoist can be used to move machinery around safely.*

*Two planks of wood bolted to the lathe feet will often turn an unmanageable mass of metal into an easily handled machine.*

*A zero volts switch is essential equipment on any machine tool.*

diagram of the electrical connections so you can rewire the lathe when you get it home. A digital camera is also a good method of recording the wiring connections, but I would not rely on the camera alone.

If the lathe does not have a zero volts switch, it would be a good idea to fit one after you get the lathe home. They are available quite cheaply and are easily fitted. If in doubt about your ability to do electrical wiring, consult a qualified electrician.

## SETTING UP THE LATHE

Some lathes, usually the larger industrial ones, have an integral bed and cabinet. The lathe can be set to true with just shimming under the feet or by adjusting the feet.

Other lathes may need to be mounted level and true to ensure accuracy when turning. Set the bench/stand as level as you can in both directions using a spirit level as a guide. Any cheap spirit level will do as long as it is accurate. You can test the accuracy of a spirit level by turning it round 180 degrees; if it is accurate it should read the same both ways.

Once the stand is reasonably level, you can level the lathe. This involves jacking

*Adjustable feet are very useful for levelling up the lathe.*

or shimming up the lathe until it is true in both directions. If using a wooden bench, put metal plates under the feet to spread the load. Shim or adjust the lathe until it is reasonably level.

Insert a length of bar in the chuck and put a dial test indicator on top of the tailstock end of the bar. Nip the headstock end mounting bolts down first and then tighten down the tailstock end bolts. Adjust or shim the tailstock end until there is no sign of movement on the test indicator. Next,

Any other large objects that can be removed and replaced later will make the lathe lighter and easier to move.

Wear old clothes when moving your lathe and have plenty of old rags to wipe off swarf and oil. Lay down old blankets or decorators' sheets inside the car and a sheet of thick cardboard, MDF or plywood to help protect the boot area when sliding the lathe into the car.

A smallish lathe can often be fitted into a standard hatchback or estate car. You may find, however, that you have to do two trips: one for the lathe and accessories and another for the cabinet the lathe stands on. To save a wasted journey, I usually try to fit the lathe cabinet in first. If I then find that the cabinet doesn't fit, I can still bring the lathe and tooling home knowing that I have to hire a van to collect the cabinet, but also that I have not had a wasted journey.

If you have to split the electrics, for example to take the lathe off the cabinet, draw a

*Put the spirit level on the cabinet's longitudinal axis and use the adjustable feet to level the lathe.*

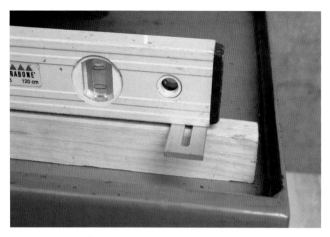

1.   Insert a piece of $^1/_8$in (3mm) packing under the spirit level at the tailstock end. This will result in a run on the drip tray and all the old oil will run to the end of the lathe, making it easier to clean up.

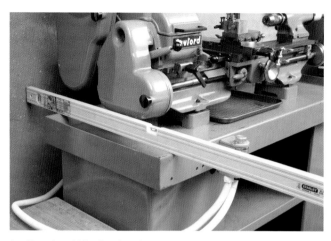

2.   Place the spirit level on the cabinet cross axis and use the adjustable feet to level the lathe.

3.   Put the spirit level on the lathe cross axis at the headstock end and level it as best you can.

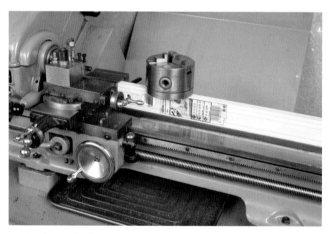

4.   Put the spirit level on the longitudinal axis and level along the lathe.

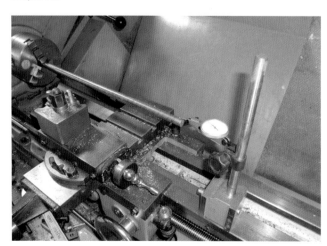

5.   Test the top of the bar; there should be no movement when the lathe is clamped down.

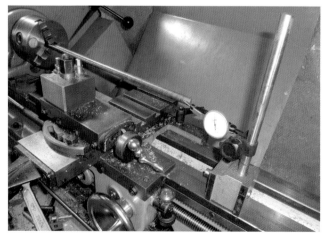

6.   Test the front of the bar, again ensuring that there is no movement when the lathe is clamped down.

*Align the tailstock by using a dial test indicator in the headstock.*

6.4. repeat the procedure with the dial test indicator on the front of the bar. Again you are looking for no movement. Check both directions again, making sure there is no movement either horizontally or vertically when you tighten the lathe down. Adjust or shim until there is no movement in either direction when the lathe is clamped down. As long as the bed is not twisted, the lathe bed should now be true.

## Aligning the Tailstock

Now we need to set the tailstock in line with the headstock. Do this by putting the dial test indicator into the headstock chuck and test the tailstock bore. Adjust the tailstock towards the front or to the back of the bed until the test indicator reads true and tighten the clamp screws. A slight difference in vertical height will not be the end of the world; it just means there is probably some wear to the base of the tailstock casting but there should be no variation from front to back in the horizontal alignment.

Put a long bar between the centres and take a light cut along it using a fine power feed. Run along the bar a couple more times at the same setting to remove any push off. When you measure the bar, it should measure the same at both ends. If the bar is larger at the tailstock end, you need to reduce the height of the bed at the front of the tailstock slightly. If smaller at the tailstock end, you need to reduce the shim at the back of the tailstock end. It probably won't need much adjustment, as slight adjustments to the shim or adjusters at the tailstock end will soon bring it into line.

## Lubricating the Lathe

You should follow the manufacturer's recommendations for lubrication. Usually this is thin oil for the headstock, often hydraulic oil, and slideway oil for the moving parts. Lubrication should be done regularly. If the lathe is fitted with a sight feed oiler, it should show oil in it. Adjustable sight feed oilers, as used on Myford and similar lathes, should be adjusted so that the oil drips when the lathe is running but does not drip much when the lathe is stopped. The slight vibration when the motor is running is usually enough to cause the oil to drip. Too much oil is better than not enough: oil is far cheaper than new bearings.

*Using a test bar to check for parallel turning.*

*A typical drip-feed lubricator.*

showing at the edge of the sliding surfaces. A squirt of oil on the cross slide and topslide feed screw bearing is needed as well. Check the manufacturer's instructions for lubricating the rest of the lathe. Follow the motor maker's recommendation for lubricating the motor.

Try to avoid using WD40 on the lathe. While it is an excellent lubricant/water displacer, it tends to discolour the lathe bed.

## Avoiding the Rust Fairy

Rust can play havoc with a lathe, quickly turning the bed and other parts into a brown mess. Various sizes of plastic covers suitable for covering lathes are often sold for use as barbecue covers in DIY stores. A plastic lathe cover will help to keep rust at bay but more needs to be done. A bag containing silica gel placed under the plastic cover, for example, will absorb excess moisture; silica gel can be bought very cheaply on eBay.

Use an oil gun on all the oil nipples. You can get around the tendency for the oil to go everywhere except into the nipple by putting a piece of writing paper over the nipple and then using the oil gun as normal. The paper will stop the oil squirting everywhere. The mandrel back gear also needs to be lubricated. When in use the main back gear is running on the outside of the lathe mandrel and needs to be lubricated often or it will get hot and wear.

Changewheels should be lubricated with oil, not grease. If you use grease, swarf will stick to the change wheels and cause unnecessary wear. To stop swarf running through the mandrel and dropping out onto the changewheels, put a wine bottle cork or similar into the left-hand end of the mandrel. This will effectively stop any swarf getting through to the change wheels.

Oil the saddle and cross slide and also the nipples on the tailstock. Make sure oil is

*Silica gel is easily obtainable from eBay.*

Alternatively, you can buy a vapour phase inhibitor for protecting the lathe. The vapour phase inhibitor chemical is supplied on a felt pad inside a plastic pot. The chemical forms a protective layer on every surface. Because it is a vapour, it will find its way into every cranny and is also used for protecting tools and accessories in tool cabinets and drawers. It usually lasts for twelve months if

*Use a bit of paper under the oil gun to stop the oil squirting everywhere.*

enclosed by the plastic cover. Some machine tool dealers are able to sell supplies of this product in small, ready to use containers rather than in industrial quantities.

Always clean the lathe down after use; swarf will soon rust if left on a lathe as it will probably be clean from turning and will not be protected by oil. The use of an oven cooking tray under the lathe bed makes it easy to remove swarf at the end of a turning session. The tray also helps to retrieve a parted off component or a lost screw from a tipped turning tool. Another alternative is to cover the lathe chip tray with newspaper; when you have finished turning, remove the newspaper, screw it up and throw it away.

When fitting a chuck or faceplate to the lathe, make sure you clean the mandrel thread, the register and the face. You should also clean the mating threads, the bore and the face on the chuck or faceplate. You can clean the thread and bore easily by using two toothbrushes bolted back to back with spacers in between. Make sure the Morse tapers in the headstock and tailstock are clean before fitting a Morse taper accessory. The Morse taper to be fitted should be free from scratches, burrs and bruises.

It is good idea to make a chuck board for use when fitting chucks to a lathe or removing them. This is a piece of wood (plywood will do) that sits on the lathe bed while you are screwing the chuck on and off. The chuck board will protect the lathe if you drop the chuck. It can also be used to protect the lathe bed when you are hacksawing or filing in the lathe.

If you keep your lathe clean and lubricate it regularly it should last a lifetime.

## SAFETY IN THE WORKSHOP

Remember, you are responsible for your own safety.

Safety is a major concern in the workshop. There are certain things you should do and, obviously, things you should not. By its very nature a workshop can be a dangerous place; all we can do is make it as safe as possible while still allowing us to work in it.

### Working Alone

Most of you reading this book will probably be working alone in a small workshop, garage or garden shed. If you get hurt, you may possibly be on your own. As a priority,

I suggest you take a mobile phone into the workshop and keep it in your pocket. The ability to contact your family, a friend or the emergency services quickly could save your life. Keep the phone switched off while in the workshop, however, as it is an unnecessary distraction.

### First Aid

A First Aid box, with contents, is a necessity and should include an eye-bath and eyewash. You should particularly learn how to stop blood flowing. There are plenty of websites that will tell you how to do this. Check them out now before you go back into the workshop.

### Electrical Safety

Check for earth continuity, while the machine is unplugged, with a volt ohmmeter from the earth pin on the three pin plug to the metal part of the lathe (some paint may have to be removed for a reading to take place). You should get a reading of zero ohms or a beep if the meter has a continuity range. You should also be sure that the electrical sockets on the wall are correctly earthed. If in doubt, consult a competent electrician.

Lighting and electric heating should be on a separate circuit to the machines, so you will still have light if the machines trip out. Plug a small light into the machine circuit so you have some light if the lighting circuit trips out. When I go on holiday, I always turn

*A large tray will catch much of the swarf and the holes let the oil drain away. Use newspaper to soak up the excess oil.*

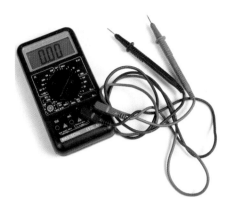

*A digital multimeter is very useful in the home workshop.*

off the fuse trips for the lighting in order to make it more difficult for intruders to move about quickly. Leave the house alarm and smoke detectors on. (The house alarm may activate eight hours after the electricity is turned off when the battery expires.)

## Be Aware

Be mentally alert while using the lathe. Avoid operations that might put your hands at risk of entering the moving parts of the lathe. Do not operate any lathe while under the influence of drugs, alcohol or prescription medication that may cause drowsiness or otherwise affect your ability to control the lathe safely. Do not attempt to work on a lathe and talk at the same time. If you have to talk to someone, switch off the lathe before doing so.

## Keep It Clean

The area around a lathe should be kept free of obstructions. The floor should be clean and dry, with any oil or other spills cleaned up immediately. The lathe should be kept clean and tidy. Machine danger areas should be marked on the workshop floor

and observed. Workbenches placed near a lathe should be strong and equipped with a non-slip safety surface to stop tools or other items rolling onto the floor; a rubber car mat will suffice. A rubber doormat on the floor will allow swarf to drop through in order to save you getting swarf embedded in the soles of your shoes.

*A suitable floor mat will allow swarf to drop through and help keep your feet warm in winter.*

## Learn to Use the Lathe

Do not use any lathe before you are familiar

with the controls and are aware of the different ways of stopping it. This may be a clutch, an on/off switch, a No Volts release switch or an emergency stop button. I strongly advise fitting a No Volts release switch if your lathe does not have one. As well as being useful for stopping the lathe in an emergency, it will prevent the lathe from starting up by itself after a power cut. If you are not comfortable working with electrical equipment, get a qualified electrician to fit the switch for you.

## Stay with the Lathe

Never ever walk away, even for a moment, while the lathe you are using is switched on. Switch it off if you are leaving it unattended and only leave the lathe after it has come to a complete stop. Never leave a lathe in an unsafe condition. Make sure that you have not left the chuck key in the chuck. The chances are that if you are halfway through setting up the lathe, when you return you will forget what you have or have not done. If in doubt, leave a big notice reminding yourself to check that the lathe is safe before continuing.

*Do not leave the chuck key in the chuck.*

## Switch Off when Adjusting the Lathe

Shut off the power supply to the motor before starting any operations requiring access to the lathe, such as changing tools, measuring work, mounting or removing accessories, changing speed and setting up change gears. The lathe must be safely stopped. Just zeroing a variable-speed drive is not safely stopping it; use the zero volts switch to switch the power off as well.

## Check before Starting the Lathe

Always rotate your workpiece by hand to make sure it clears the tool rest, saddle and bed. Double check to make sure your work is securely clamped in the chuck or between centres before starting the lathe. Be certain that the workpiece turns freely and is firmly mounted.

The speed of the lathe must be checked before turning it on. When turning irregular shapes, start the lathe on a low speed and increase the speed by a pulley step each time. If the lathe is bouncing about, lower the speed and/or balance the work. If the work vibrates, stop the lathe and check the reason. The chances are that you are running the lathe too fast.

Measuring equipment, tooling and workpieces should not be left on a lathe as they can vibrate off into moving components and be thrown around the room. Check for loose items on a lathe before use.

## Use the Lathe Guards

New lathes will be fitted with guards over the motor shaft, drive belt and spindle pulleys. These guards should always be in place before using the lathe. Any other moving parts should be guarded to prevent anything falling onto the moving parts.

Although guards are often removed by machinists, provided they are constructed from clear materials and open and close easily, they add safety without interfering with the work being done. Guards will, at the same time, deflect swarf and any coolant that is being used. Guards fitted to the lathe should not be removed while it is in use. They should be made from suitable material and not have sharp edges. They should not be removed for adjustment and lubrication of the lathe unless this is unavoidable. Lathe manufacturers don't usually supply chip guards, so adding one should be considered. Chip guards with magnetic bases are available although they can attract steel swarf to the magnet. Put the base into a plastic bag to aid swarf removal.

## Use Eye Protection

Lathes can throw sharp metal chips considerable distances, especially at high cutting speeds. Apart from deep cuts, the chips may leave the tool red hot, cause skin burns and even burn holes in clothing. You must use safety goggles or proper safety spectacles while in the workshop. Always wear industrial quality safety glasses fitted with side-shields. Spectacles without safety lenses are not adequate eye protection. When the glasses get dirty, do not wipe them off as they will become scratched. Wash them off under the tap instead.

## Take Care when Removing Swarf

Do not attempt to remove chips or turnings with your hands. Always switch off the lathe first and either pull the swarf away with a large metal hook or lift it off using a pair of gloves. If the swarf is tangled around the lathe, untangle it with a pair of pliers and not a gloved hand, as it will cut straight through the gloves and into your hand. Use a dustpan and brush to remove small chips and swarf from the swarf tray – never use your hands. When swarf becomes stringy and builds up on the tool or tool post, turn off the lathe before removing it.

## Avoid Loose Clothing

If you are not wearing overalls, wear short-sleeved shirts or roll long shirt sleeves above the elbows. Loose sleeves can catch on rotating work and quickly pull your hand or arm into the lathe. Obviously, though, keep your arms protected if hot swarf is flying around.

Swarf can get inside protective clothing, especially collars (use a clothes peg to keep your collar tight), pockets and shoes. To stop the sleeves of an overall catching, sew elastic into the cuffs or wrap a couple of thick elastic bands around the cuffs to stop the sleeves getting caught up.

Under no circumstances wear a necktie when operating a lathe. Protective gloves should never be worn while operating a lathe. Protective gloves may be worn when swarf is being removed but they must be removed before switching the lathe back on.

## Use Sturdy Footwear

Wear steel toecap safety boots; they are not expensive and will help to protect your feet from injury if you drop a heavy object on them. The 'trainer' version is particularly comfortable. Do not allow stringy swarf to fall on the floor, as you will get cuts on your ankles and may even trip over it.

## Avoid Jewellery

Do not wear wristwatches, rings or jewellery when in the workshop as it could catch on a rotating part of the lathe or workpiece. This also applies when moving a lathe into or out of the workshop, since they could catch on a falling lathe. If your other half complains that you have taken off your wedding ring, explain that you wouldn't be able to wear it again if your finger is missing due to an accident. Long hair should be tied back, as you could be pulled into the lathe if it gets caught in the rotating work.

## Lifting in the Workshop

Back injuries can be caused by incorrect lifting practices. It is important to bend your legs when lifting rather than bending your back. A hoist or engine lift should be used to lift heavy items. A stool in the workshop will take the pressure off your legs and will provide a welcome break after you have been stood at the lathe for a while.

## Self-igniting Materials

If you machine titanium or magnesium, which can ignite and burn vigorously, keep the accumulation of turnings to a minimum. If the material does catch fire, don't use water or a water-based coolant as an extinguisher, since it will make matters much worse. Before starting to machine titanium or magnesium, fill a large bucket with dry sand, cover it and keep it by the lathe. The sand will smother the flames very effectively. You could also buy one of the special fire retardants used in industry.

Beware also of grinding aluminium on the bench grinder. Aluminium and steel filings are the ingredients of Thermite, a powerful explosive that can also burn. If you grind aluminium and then change over to grinding steel, the red hot sparks are liable to set the steel/aluminium mix on fire. This is a very dangerous combination of materials and should be avoided at all costs.

## Safety with Bar Stock

Bar stock should be contained within the headstock and not allowed to protrude from the rear of the mandrel. I once saw someone switch on a lathe when a brass bar was sticking out from the back of the headstock by about two feet. With the lathe running at 2,000rpm, the bar, which was about ¾in (19 mm) in diameter, was bent at right angles and caused the heavy lathe, which weighed 1,280kg, to jump about. Luckily someone managed to switch the lathe off before any major damage occurred. It was not the operator: he had run well away and was nowhere to be seen.

## Some Final Words on Safety

Wherever possible the machine height should be adjusted to suit the user. We are still using fifty-year-old machines, but fifty years ago the nation was shorter.

The workplace should be provided with uniform lighting that gives an adequate level of illumination. Individual machine lights are best.

The lathe must be set to operate at the speeds and feeds recommended for the specific metal being turned. If the metal rotates too slowly or too quickly, or the feed is too slow or too fast, accidents are likely to occur.

The area directly in front of and behind the workpiece is known as the 'firing zone' or the 'red zone'. This is where a piece of work is likely to go as it leaves the lathe. Make it a habit to keep clear of this zone when you turn the lathe on. Learn where the No Volts switch is as you might need to turn the lathe off quickly.

By following all the above advice you should now be able to work safely, fully aware of any safety problems that might arise.

At this point you now know how to install the lathe, look after it, clean it and maintain it. In Chapter 3 we will look at cutting tools and examine how to select cutting speeds and feeds.

*This bar is sticking out too far from the back of the lathe.*

# 3   *Cutting Tool Principles, Feeds and Speeds*

The first part of this chapter will look at the materials from which cutting tools are made, as well as their basic shape and geometry. We will then consider selecting suitable speeds and feeds.

## MAIN TYPES OF TURNING TOOLS

There are three main types of turning tool used in modern workshops: HSS (high speed steel) tools, carbide brazed-on tools and inserted tip tools. All have their uses in the workshop and for most jobs there is no preference for one type over the others. There are also carbon steel tool bits, although in practice they are just about obsolete. Carbon steel tools can be made in the home workshop, but apart from being used to make form tools (see Chapter 11), the reader is unlikely to use this material for tools.

## HSS Tools

HSS tools can be purchased singly or in sets already ground to the correct shape.

It is cheaper, however, to purchase them as square tool blanks in various sizes ready for you to grind to shape. The complete ready-ground sets will probably come with several shapes included that you will never use. If you can buy a few ready-ground tools cheaply, they will be of use as guides to see how to sharpen your own HSS tool blanks.

HSS form tools from industry are often available second-hand. These are especially ground to machine a complex form all in one go. You can often find some that are ground to a suitable shape to form the end of a threaded component, including the undercut.

## Brazed-on Carbide Tools

Brazed-on carbide-tipped tools are quite useful, especially for facing and boring cast iron, but they really need a diamond-faced grinding wheel to keep them sharp. Carbide tips and tools come in various sizes and hardness to suit individual materials: carbide tools for steel will often be painted

*HSS form turning tools.*

blue, those for cast iron are painted red and those for stainless steel are painted yellow. The colour indicates the suitability of the tool for certain materials.

## Inserted Tip Tools

Inserted carbide tip tools are very useful but they are not cheap. The tips are not usually sharpened after wearing out; you just throw the tip away and fit a new one. Most modern

*A general-purpose HSS turning tool suitable for mild steel.*

*Brazed-on carbide-tipped tools come in various grades, shapes and sizes.*

*The left-hand tool is blue, indicating it is for mild steel, while the right-hand tool is red, indicating it is for turning cast iron.*

carbide inserts, however, do have more than one cutting face; sometimes they have two and occasionally four or more cutting edges are available. You can even get form turning tools where the insert is round and can be rotated a full 360 degrees.

Some diamond-shaped tips can be used in different tool holders: two edges are used in one tool holder and the other two edges are used in another tool holder, so you get twice the life per tip.

Inserted tip tools are available for internal and external screwcutting where the tips are held at the correct helix angle of the thread in the tool holder. The drawback is the cost of the tips and each size of thread usually needs its own size of tip.

*An inserted tip carbide turning tool.*

### Carbide grooving tools

Inserted tip grooving tools are ideal for machining grooves for O rings and circlips. They are available in many standard widths and can often be used as parting-off tools for smaller diameters. One of the most useful grooving tools for smaller size grooves and parting off is the Mini Thin system as sold by MSC Industrial Supply Co.

*The Mini Thin tool holder is ideal for grooving and also for parting off small diameters. The shank is so strong compared with the cut being taken that using an overhang, as shown, is quite safe.*

### Coatings to reduce tool wear

Tips are also available with various coatings that improve tool life. The most common coating is titanium nitride (TiN), which is gold in colour. Other coatings that offer slightly better wear resistance are titanium carbon nitride (TiCN), which is blue grey in colour, and titanium aluminium nitride (TiAlN), which is violet bronze. Ready-ground HSS cutting tools, such as drills, taps and reamers, are also available with these coatings but once you sharpen the cutter, the coating is gone.

Tipped tools need a deeper cut, a higher feed and a higher speed than HSS tools. This

means that the lathe needs to be strong, rigid and have ample power to drive the lathe mandrel when taking a heavy cut; this rules out using tipped tools on lathes smaller than about 2in (50mm) centre height.

Smaller tools are made to fit the Unimat and similar small lathes, but these machines just don't have the power needed to drive them. At best taking a cut will stop the lathe; at worst the tool will chip.

### Inserted tip types

Inserted tip tools come in many shapes and sizes. Some tip shapes and sizes are made to an international standard and others are to the maker's own standards. Wherever possible, use ISO standard tools as the tips will be interchangeable with those from other manufacturers and will probably be cheaper as well. The ANSI system commonly used in the USA is not compatible with the ISO system used in the rest of the world.

If your lathe is powerful enough, you can take advantage of inserted tip parting off blades. These are mounted in a special tool block and the blade can be slid in or out, depending on the diameter you are parting off. The blade carries an inserted tip specially designed for parting off. There are three types of tip available: square-ended tips, tips that are angled to the left and tips that are angled to the right. Square tips are used for general parting off; tips angled to the left are used when you don't want to leave a pip on the back end of the work; and tips angled to the right are used when you want a clean face on the front of the work.

The parting off blade is often mounted upside down at the back of the lathe cross slide. The action of parting off tends to lift the whole cross slide slightly and forces the cross slide tightly into the matching dovetail, which makes it much more rigid. If the parting off tool digs in while in the back tool post the tool tends to lift and push

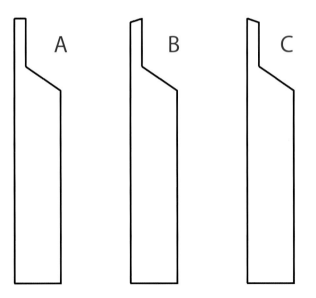

*Simplified diagram of parting off tool angles: (A) straight parting tool; (B) angled to the left; (C) angled to the right.*

intermittent cuts, and because in industrial use carbide tips are called on to remove larger quantities of metal at higher speeds and feeds.

For guidance on using tipped tools in the small workshop, where time is not as important as in an industrial environment, I would recommend using twice the speed used for normal HSS tools and a fine feed of about 0.002in (0.05mm) per rev as a starting point. This can be adjusted up or down depending on the results. The main difference between HSS tools and carbide tipped tools (either brazed-on or inserted tip) is the horse power requirement of the machine in use.

## SELECTING THE CORRECT SPEEDS FOR DIFFERENT MATERIALS

Over many years, through trial and error, cutting speeds have been determined that give an optimum tool life balanced with a decent surface finish. These speeds are normally quoted in 'surface speed in feet per minute'.

Speeds and feeds used on industrial machines, where the primary tools will have inserted tips, will be a lot higher than those used in the small workshop where HSS tools are the norm.

The accompanying table gives an idea of the speeds that should be used for various common types of material likely to be found in the workshop. The speeds listed should be suitable for both turning and drilling in the lathe. For reaming use about 25 per cent of the recommended speeds.

The table is a guide only and it is likely that the machine speeds available will not be exactly those required and you may have to resort to 'near enough is good enough'. Set the lathe to the nearest speed lower than indicated in the table for the diameter and material being cut. This will be fine for HSS tools.

Double the recommended HSS speed for carbide tools. For parting off use about

away from the work, whereas in a front tool post the tool tends to dig in and pull into the work.

## POWER REQUIREMENTS

When turning mild steel or stainless steel with any carbide tool, the machine horse power required is considerably more than that required for ordinary HSS tools. The two main reasons for this are that carbide tools often have a negative rake angle on the cutting edge, as this type of edge lasts much longer than a positive angle, especially for

*This parting off tool is mounted at the back of the lathe in a special back tool holder.*

| Material, Cutter or Drill Diameter In millimetres | Carbon Steel Stainless Steel Alloy Steels | Cast Iron | Phosphor Bronze Gunmetal | Mild Steel | Copper Hard Brass | Aluminium Soft Brass Nickel Silver |
|---|---|---|---|---|---|---|
| | 15 Metres Per Minute 50 Feet Per Minute | 18 Metres Per Minute 60 Feet Per Minute | 24 Metres Per Minute 80 Feet Per Minute | 30 Metres Per Minute 100 Feet per Minute | 45 Metres Per Minute 150 Feet Per Minute | 60 Metres Per Minute 200 Feet Per Minute |
| 250 | 19 | 23 | 31 | 38 | 57 | 76 |
| 225 | 21 | 25 | 34 | 42 | 64 | 85 |
| 200 | 24 | 29 | 38 | 48 | 72 | 96 |
| 175 | 27 | 33 | 44 | 55 | 82 | 109 |
| 150 | 32 | 38 | 51 | 64 | 96 | 127 |
| 125 | 38 | 46 | 61 | 76 | 115 | 153 |
| 100 | 48 | 57 | 76 | 96 | 143 | 191 |
| 75 | 64 | 76 | 102 | 127 | 191 | 255 |
| 50 | 96 | 115 | 153 | 191 | 287 | 382 |
| 25 | 191 | 229 | 306 | 382 | 1461 | 764 |
| 19 | 251 | 302 | 402 | 503 | 754 | 1006 |
| 16 | 299 | 358 | 478 | 1902 | 896 | 1194 |
| 12 | 398 | 478 | 637 | 796 | 1194 | 1592 |
| 10 | 478 | 573 | 764 | 955 | 1433 | 1911 |
| 8 | 597 | 717 | 955 | 1194 | 1791 | 2389 |
| 6 | 796 | 955 | 1274 | 1592 | 2389 | 3185 |

30 per cent of the recommended HSS speed. For form tools, use about 50 per cent of the recommended speed for the initial cuts and then engage the corresponding back gear (just switch to back gear leaving the belts on the same pulley) and gently tap the handle until it reaches the finished size and allow it to finish the cut by itself. You may have to adjust the speed down if you get a lot of chatter.

For turning cast iron, use a carbide-tipped tool running at the HSS speed to remove the skin. You can then finish the turning with a HSS steel tool if you wish.

Please remember, if doing any work that might be unbalanced, start off slowly and increase the speed a belt step at a time.

## THE ACTION OF CUTTING TOOLS

Basically a lathe tool is a wedge that is forced into the end of the rotating bar to remove metal. As long as the tool is fed forward while the lathe is rotating, material will be removed.

A typical right-hand turning tool has a cutting angle of 90 degrees less the side clearance, less the side rake. The cutting angle for this example is 90–10–10 = 70 degrees. This is the angle that is wedged into the work to remove the material. Softer materials will have a smaller cutting angle, while harder materials will have a larger cutting angle. Tool angles vary depending on the type of metal being turned. Tools for turning softer metals usually have higher rake angles than those designed for harder metals, since a turning tool will normally hold its edge for longer in softer materials. Brass, although soft, usually has no top rake on the tool at all.

Other angles to be aware of are the top rake and the side rake.

## CUTTING TOOL SHAPES

The following are some of the different shapes that you might find useful for general turning and metal removal.

**Right-hand knife tool.** This is used for general turning and facing of bar stock. Depending on the work you are doing, you may find a left-hand version of this tool useful.

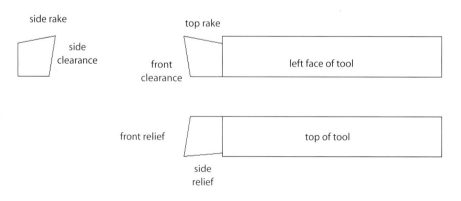

*Right-hand knife turning tool. All rake angles are 10 degrees.*

**Right-hand roughing tool.** It has a leading angle and a small radius on the tip of the tool. This tool is used for fast metal removal where finish is not too important. Again, you may find a left-hand version useful.

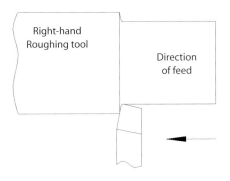

*Typical roughing tool.*

A roughing tool cutting at an angle to a bar will remove a chip wider and thinner than a tool cutting at 90 degrees to the bar. This improves tool life, although you will have to square the turning up with a standard knife tool.

**Double-sided roughing tool.** It can turn towards the left or right. It can also be used as a plunge tool to remove material from a groove or where the component needs to be 'waisted' down.

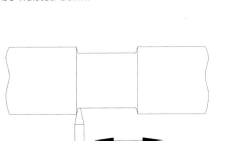

*Typical double-sided roughing tool.*

**Simple parting off tool.** This is suitable for most materials. You will probably need a large one for parting off large diameter bars as well as a small one for parting off small components.

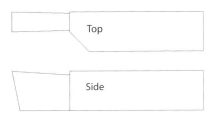

*Simple parting off tool.*

**Screwcutting tool.** This is used for cutting screw threads. The angle will depend on the thread you are cutting: 60 degrees for metric, 55 degrees for Whitworth and BSF etc.

*Internal (top) and external (bottom) screwcutting tools.*

**Boring and facing tool.** This tool's unusual shape will be found very useful when recessing a large bore. It will plunge straight into a small drilled hole and will also face right across the bottom of the recess.

*Shallow boring tool capable of facing across the bottom of a hole.*

**Double-ended chamfering tool.** It has 45 degree angles at both ends so it can be used to chamfer external diameters and internal bores.

*Double-ended chamfer tool chamfering a diameter.*

*Double-ended chamfer tool chamfering a bore.*

Other shapes can be useful but the tools shown here should be sufficient to get you going.

## BORING TOOLS

Boring tools are used to clean up a previously drilled hole, possibly to make it run true but more likely to ensure the hole is to the correct size. They are normally longer than ordinary tools and tend to stick out further from the tool holder. HSS tools are suitable for most uses. Carbide inserted tip boring bars are also readily available and are the best bet for turning cast iron in the small workshop.

*A small carbide boring bar inserted into a mild steel shank.*

*HSS boring bar.*

For really small holes, down to 2 or 3mm in diameter, solid HSS and carbide boring bars are readily available. Although they are not cheap, they will be found very useful and quick to use.

Another method of boring a hole is to use a long series slot drill as a boring tool. In use, clamp the shank in the tool holder with the point at centre height, making sure the rest of the slot drill is clear of the side of the bore. You can then run it through the bore in a similar manner to a standard boring bar.

## PARTING OFF TOOLS

Parting off tools provide a quick way of cutting off work from the parent bar. There is rarely any need to worry about cutting the component off to the correct length to get a good finish. As long as the component is longer than required it can be put back into the chuck or a collet and the parted off face can be faced to length or otherwise worked on.

The parting off tool cutting face can either be square or it can be angled to the left or right (*see* page 43).

The side of the parting off tool could even be radiused so that it forms a radius on the end of the next component or chamfered to form a lead-in edge for the next tool.

## CUTTING LUBRICANTS

To make cutting tools cut easily and to pro-

long their life, it is sometimes best to use a cutting lubricant. For steel I prefer neat cutting oil. It lubricates but is not ideal for cooling the work.

In industry coolant is normally used. This is oil that has an additive to make it soluble in water. Most soluble oils will do, but the synthetic ones tend to sting your hands if you have any open cuts. I would not recommend using soluble oils on the home workshop lathe as I think they tend to wash the lubricating oil off the slideways and can encourage rust. However, this is my personal preference and many people use soluble oil in the home workshop without any problems.

Oil is suitable for use when cutting steels, mild steels, stainless steels and high carbon steels such as silver steel.

The best lubricant when cutting aluminium is paraffin. It stops the aluminium from building up on the cutting tool.

Brass and cast iron are normally cut dry. When turning cast iron on a lathe, if the lathe is fitted with a soluble oil tank, the cast iron dust will have an affinity for the soluble oil. If the lathe is then used on aluminium the free carbon in the cast iron can contaminate the aluminium with black streaks.

I normally place the oil or paraffin in a small dish (actually a cat or dog food bowl) and apply it by hand with a small brush. This does all I need.

The next chapter looks at grinding lathe tools.

# 4 Sharpening Tools and Holding Them in the Lathe

The next task is to grind a set of useful lathe tools.

The first thing you will need is an off-hand grinder. The grinder can be a dangerous machine so it should be used with care. Eye protection must be worn, the guards should be correctly fitted and there must be adequate illumination. I don't like using a grinder in a small workshop as the grinding dust flies everywhere and can get onto the machine slideways and tools, generally making the workshop dusty and dirty. If possible, set up the grinder in a separate area away from the workshop; I have my grinder mounted on a food chopping board so I can carry it outside to use. This has the added benefit of daylight, although you are dependent on the weather or you might need to use it after dark.

## GRINDING WHEELS

It has always been stated that you should never grind a tool on the side of the grinding wheel. So, following this theory, we will be using a recessed wheel where its width is much thicker than the part of the wheel used to clamp the wheel to the grinder. I struggled to find a recessed wheel of 6in (150mm) diameter and finally found a 60 grit grinding wheel on a personal visit to Axminster Power Tools in Devon. (I could find only an 80 grit wheel in their catalogue.) The wheels I like to use for grinding are A60K5V, if I can get them, and I prefer the white wheels designed for the harder tool steels rather than the grey or brown wheels, which are more suitable for softer mild steels. The designation breaks down like this: A stands for aluminium oxide; 60 is the grit size; K is the hardness (I, J and K being medium hard); 5 is the structure (the space between grains of grit); and V is for vitrified, the method of bonding the grains together. The K and the 5 can vary a bit either way and the grit should be 46, 60 or 80, with 60 being preferred. The 80 grit is a bit fine and will clog up quite quickly.

So-called green grit wheels made from silicon carbide are available for sharpening carbide tools. They are usually softer than aluminium oxide wheels in order to allow the grit to break down before the wheel becomes glazed from grinding the much harder carbide.

*The guard of this off-hand grinder has been widened to accept a recessed wheel.*

*With a recessed wheel you can cut on the outer face of the recessed side of the wheel.*

## Testing the Wheel

The first thing you should do when buying a wheel is to make sure that it is rated at a sufficiently high speed for the grinder on which it is to be used. Off-hand grinders usually run at around 2,900rpm, so you will need a wheel rated to at least that speed; it is all the better if the grinding wheel is rated at a higher speed than the grinder. Care should be taken when handling grinding wheels as they are quite fragile if knocked or dropped. A grinding wheel should only be purchased from a reputable engineering supplier. Support your grinding wheel on a piece of wood and tap the wheel gently with a plastic screwdriver handle or similar. The wheel should 'ring'; if it sounds dull, it should be broken in half and either thrown away or used on the workbench as a sharpening stone. Never throw a wheel away without breaking it into two; you never know who might get their hands on it.

## Mounting the Wheel

The wheel's bore should be the same as the spindle of the grinding wheel. Often the bore will be larger and you will then need some plastic spacers to reduce it. Spacers should be readily available from your local engineering supplier. You can turn the spacers from plastic if you can't buy any ready-made ones.

At each side of the wheel you should fit a paper washer; these are made of blotting paper type material and will probably have been supplied already stuck on the wheel. The grinder should have two metal flanges, one to fit at each side of the wheel. Both flanges should be the same diameter. These will hold the wheel true and spread the tightening load on the wheel. The grinder will have two different threads on the ends of its spindle. The right-hand side of the grinder will have a right-hand thread and the left-hand side will have a left-hand thread. The different threads are to stop the clamping nuts from unscrewing when the grinder is running.

To fit the wheel, remove the guard and undo the nut. Remove the metal flange and then the wheel. Make sure the flanges don't have any remains of the old paper washer on them. Put the new wheel onto the grinder spindle (remember the spacer, the paper washers and the flanges at either side) and screw the nut hand-tight. Finally, hold the wheel gently and give the nut a pinch up with a spanner. You don't need to over-tighten the nut, just sufficiently to stop the wheel from coming loose. Refit the guard and spin the wheel by hand to ensure it is not rubbing anywhere. Now we are almost ready to switch the grinder on. Before doing so, however, put on your eye protection and stand to one side of the grinder so you are not in line with the wheel should it burst. Then switch the grinder on. All should be fine and the wheel should be rotating safely.

## TOOL REST

The work rest supplied with an off-hand

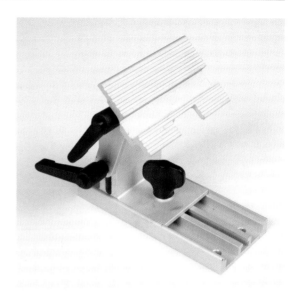

*This tool rest was designed to sharpen plane irons and chisels, but it is fine for lathe tools.*

*A modern digital angle gauge is ideal for setting the tool rest.*

*Sheet metal protractors are available very cheaply.*

grinder is usually just a bit of bent sheet metal bolted on. It is usable but only just.

I recently purchased a ready-made tool rest as a basis for making an improved grinding rest. This was originally designed for sharpening plane blades and chisels for woodworking, but it makes an ideal rest for sharpening lathe tools. It is made of aluminium and is fully adjustable for angle. The best method of setting the rest to the correct angle is to use a digital angle gauge. These are now very cheap and are readily obtainable. The position of the rest, in relation to the grinding wheel, can be adjusted on its sliding base. Many designs for tool rests have been published and you could make one of those instead if you wish to save money.

The tool clamp as supplied is designed to clamp plane irons and chisels, so this needs to be changed. Lathe tools need to be presented to the grinding wheel at the correct angles. If you don't have a digital angle gauge this can be achieved using simple guides made from angle, sheet metal

and some screws. I used gauge plate made from a high carbon steel with an accurate ground finish that can be hardened and tempered, but mild steel would be perfectly suitable if you don't have any gauge plate available.

You will find a protractor useful; you can

get a steel one with an adjustable blade for a reasonable price. The protractor will be used to set the tool angle that is ground on the tools.

## LATHE TOOL GEOMETRY

Lathe tools need to be ground to certain angles but the angles don't have to be exact. For most tools, somewhere handy will do unless you are grinding a form tool to a particularly accurate shape. It has been normal for books to show the angles on tools as used in a production environment where tools will ideally have a long life; often this life is calculated as lasting an eight-hour shift so the tool only has to be sharpened and reset once a day.

In the home workshop we can increase these cutting angles and get better cutting at the slight expense of shorter tool life.

We have already explained the shapes of the tools that you will find most useful. Tool angles are known by technical terms: top rake, front rake, side rake and back rake. The rake angles vary depending on the material to be machined, but a set of standard tools will get you started. Some of the accompanying photographs are actually of large-scale wooden models.

*The left-hand tool is suitable for both facing and turning; the right-hand tool is suitable for turning only.*

*Left-hand side of the turning tool, showing the front clearance and the top rake.*

*Left-hand side of the facing and turning tool, showing the front and top rake.*

*Top of the facing and turning tool, showing the front and side relief.*

*Top of the turning tool, showing the front and side clearance and the top rake.*

## GRINDING A TOOL

When grinding HSS tools, try to keep them as cool as possible. If an HSS tool becomes too hot and is then quenched in water, minute cracks will form on the cutting edges. These cracks will make the tool cutting edge break down very quickly when used. The best practice is to grind a little bit off the tool and then quench it while slightly warm. Do not let the tool get hot: dip it in the water little and often. This should ensure the tool edge does not break down in use.

## Grinding Your First Tool

Most angles can be ground by using the tilting table, while others may need to be fixed in relation to the periphery of the grinding wheel. The front and side of the tool can be ground by tipping the table at the correct angle, whereas the top rake can be ground on the periphery of the wheel.

The grinder should first be switched off and unplugged. Set the tool rest to the required angle using the digital angle gauge, or an angle template, and tighten up the rest.

Before switching on the grinder, ensure that everything is free to rotate by spinning the grinding wheel by hand.

If all is well, put on your safety glasses and switch on the grinder. Place the tool on the tool rest up against the side of the protractor. Slide the tool along the table until it reaches the grinding wheel and metal starts to be removed. Slide the tool backwards and forwards slowly along the rest, while putting a little light pressure on the tool so that it continues to press against the grinding wheel.

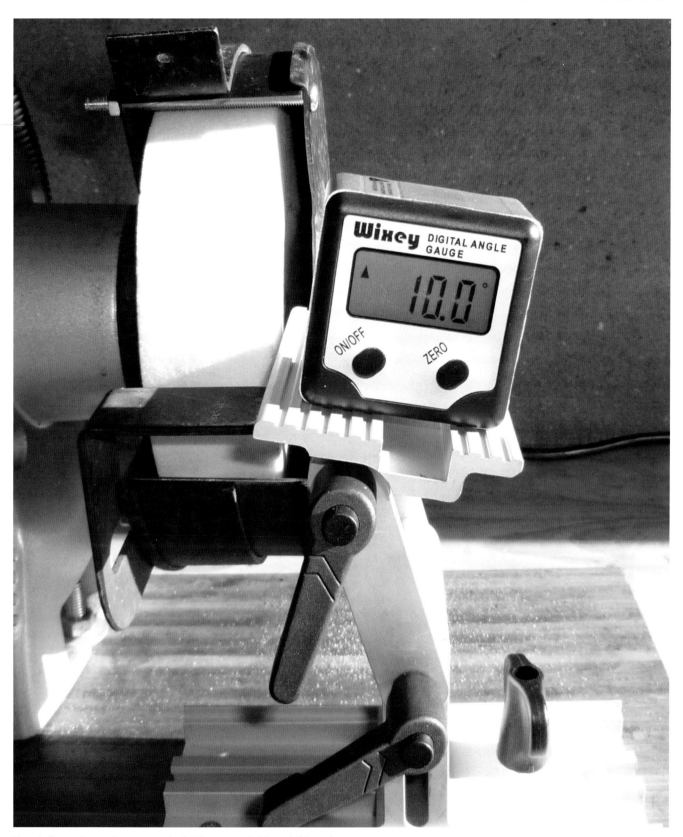

*The grinding rest is set to the correct angle of 10 degrees to grind the end of the tool.*

When you have removed a small amount of material, cool the tool bit down. At no time allow the tool bit to get hot. Continue grinding until you have removed sufficient material from the tool bit.

Turn the tool to the other angle and do the same so that now both the front and side clearance angles have been ground.

This tool will be enough for brass, but for steel we need to grind the top rake. When

*The first angle has been ground.*

grinding the top rake on a right-hand tool the slide rest needs to be higher than the centre of the grinding wheel, so that it grinds the tool at approximately 10 degrees.

You have now ground your first lathe tool. The tool as received from the grinder will be too rough to use, however, so you will need to hone the cutting edges. You can do this on an oil stone (used with fine oil like 3 in 1) or with a diamond lap, or using a combination of the two. Lightly lap the front and side clearance angles until you get a good finish and lightly hone a very small radius on the tip of the tool. Finally hone the top rake angle and your tool is ready for use.

*Grinding the first angle.*

*The second angle has been ground.*

*Grinding the second angle.*

All of your HSS turning tools can be done in this way. Only the angles will vary and these can be set using a digital angle gauge and protractor. An occasional hone will resharpen your tools as long as you treat them with care.

A similar range of HSS tools and a parting off tool, all with zero top rake, should be available if you will be turning brass. Unless you are doing quantity production, one tool holder should be sufficient for brass. As a tool for brass has no top rake and you would not normally grind the top away, as long as you buy tool steel of the same size the tip height will remain the same. You can then use the different tools in one holder without having to reset the height.

## MACHINING CAST IRON

Carbide-tipped tools are ideal for machining cast iron. A simple brazed up cranked

*Grinding the third angle.*

*The third angle has been ground.*

tool with a small chamfer on the nose will do for both turning and facing cast iron components. The main use of this tool will, however, probably be truing up the face-plate that comes with the lathe. The large diameter combined with the intermittent cut over the bolt grooves would destroy an HSS tool in a few seconds. A small tipped boring bar will be ideal for tasks like boring cast iron cylinders.

To sharpen tipped tools you need a diamond wheel or, if you want to remove large amounts of carbide, a silicon carbide wheel, often called a green grit wheel owing to its usual colour. Silicon carbide wheels are much softer than aluminium oxide wheels as they need to break down faster to present new, sharper grains to the carbide tool.

*A simple diamond lap.*

A diamond wheel is only designed to lightly lap a tipped tool; it is not suitable for removing large amounts of carbide.

*Diamond cup wheel.*

*Quick-change tool block.*

## TOOL HOLDING

Smaller lathes, such as are found in most workshops, may have a top slide with a tool clamp for individual tools, a block with a single slot to take the tool, a four-way turret (or sometimes a three-way) or a quick-change tool block and holder set. There is also the so-called American tool post, which is a round bar with a slot through it and a bolt in the top to clamp the tool. It usually comes with matching dished washers to adjust the tool height. This type is no longer very common on lathes.

### Quick-change Tool Post

The most versatile tool holding system is the quick-change tool block with matching holders. The drawback with this system is the cost of extra tool holders; you need quite a few, one for each tool.

The quick-change tool block mounts on the front of the lathe, normally on top of the top slide. (Blocks can be fitted directly on the cross slide by the use of a raising block to aid rigidity.)

Each holder is set up with its own particular tool. The tool holders can be individually set so that the turning tool is dead on centre height and is presented correctly to the workpiece.

Quick-change tool holders are available

*Quick-change tool holder.*

*Back of a quick-change tool holder, showing the dovetail type of mounting.*

*Standard tool holder with a Vee to take round tool holders.*

*Right-hand and left-hand extended tool holders.*

*Front parting off tool holder.*

with a straight cut slot to take standard square shank tool holders, with a straight cut with the addition of a Vee cut-out in the bottom for use with round tools such as boring bars, and as a front parting off tool holder to take a high speed steel parting off blade. Rear parting off tool holders are available to take an inverted parting off blade, either a high speed steel blade or an inserted tip blade. Left-handed and right-handed extended tool holders are also available and may occasionally be quite useful.

The tool block is normally mounted on the top slide but you can get raising blocks to use instead of the top slide. This makes the tool holder block much more rigid. A back quick-change tool block will need mounting on a raising block.

## Tool Clamp

Satisfactory work can be done with a tool clamped onto the top slide using shim steel to set the centre height of the tool. The main drawbacks are that you lose the position of the tool when you take it off the topslide to fit the next tool and you also lose the accurate centre height of the tool unless you keep the tool and shims together. If you are making only one component this is not a problem, but it is a nuisance if you are making a batch of matching components.

*Simple tool clamp.*

## Single-slot Block Tool Post

A block tool post is often supplied with the cheaper lathes. The tool post is literally a block of metal with a slot cut in it to take the turning tool. It is relatively easy to set the tool up at the correct centre height by using various thicknesses of shim. This is fine for the beginner to turning who is just starting out, but it is best to replace it with a four-way tool post or a quick-change tool post. You could, of course, make several block tool posts and keep each one set with a different tool.

## Four-way Tool Post

The four-way toolpost is a good compromise on a lathe as you can set four tools in the turret and rotate each one into position as needed. This speeds up production and is a lot faster than using a simple tool clamp. The drawback is that the tools stick out of the turret four different ways and you might catch your hand on a sharp tool. A simple ratchet stop ensures that each tool repeats its position when the tool post is rotated so the work is accurately turned each time the tool is used. A duplicate four-way tool post with tools for brass will speed up production

*Four-way tool post.*

*Back tool post.*

even more. Castings are available to make your own three-way tool post. The three-way tool post has the advantage of being able to get close to the work when you are turning between centres.

For the front tool post I would recommend right-hand and left-hand roughing tools, right-hand and left-hand finishing tools, a tool ground up to face bars while using a half centre, and a Mini Thin inserted tip grooving tool with grooving and parting off inserts. You will also need large and small boring bars, both HSS and with inserted tips. The HSS tools should be ground up for use as general-purpose turning tools for mild steel and similar materials. The carbide inserted tip boring bar should be fine for cast iron.

## Back Tool Post

You can fit a quick-change tool block to the back of the cross slide as well as the front. Special holders are available to take a HSS parting off blade or an inserted tip parting off blade. The blade will be angled down to give top clearance when parting off. These back-mounted tool blocks are very handy as they can also be fitted into tool holders with a facing tool or a chamfering tool.

For a back tool holder set-up I would recommend an HSS parting off blade, a facing tool for cast iron and a double-ended 45-degree chamfering tool that can be mounted parallel with the chuck or at 90 degrees to it. This set-up will allow you to face a workpiece, chamfer the outside diameter and/or the bore and part it off to length.

The next chapter looks at holding work in a chuck.

# 5 Workholding in the Chuck

This chapter covers the different types of chucks, how to use them and set up work in them accurately.

## USING CHUCKS

The most useful tools for workholding in the lathe are three- and four-jaw chucks. The three-jaw chuck is usually of the self-centring variety; this type of chuck comes as standard with two sets of jaws. The first set of jaws are known as inside or drill jaws as they are most useful for holding round and hexagon bars. The other set of jaws are outside jaws, which hold work, usually in disc form, on the outside.

Self-centring means that when you insert a bit of bar into the chuck and turn the chuck key, the chuck centralizes the workpiece as it tightens up. It is unlikely to run perfectly true, but it should run true within 3 or 4 thou.

You can also purchase soft jaws, which are exactly as their name suggests. You can then bore them out to fit the work. If you bore them on the lathe you are going to use them on, the work will run dead true.

*A set of soft jaws can be turned or bored to suit the work to be held.*

*A self-centring three-jaw chuck fitted with 'drill jaws'. Note the external jaws, which are interchangeable with the drill jaws.*

Self-centring four-jaw chucks can be used for square bars. They are also useful for holding round bars with more grip than a three-jaw self-centring chuck. Soft jaws

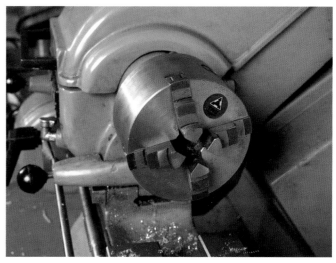

*A self-centring four-jaw chuck. These also come with external jaws and soft jaws are usually available.*

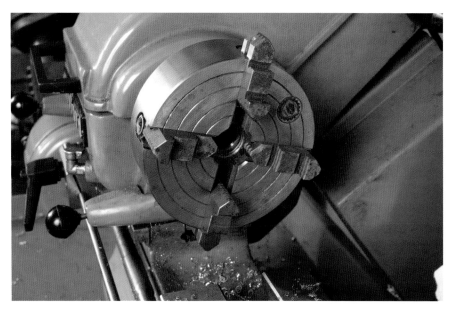

A four-jaw independent chuck.

are also available for four-jaw self-centring chucks.

You are, however, much more likely to come across a four-jaw independent chuck than a four-jaw self-centring chuck. Independent means that the jaws can be moved individually and the jaws can also be reversed: one, two, three or four of them depending on the work to be done.

A base plate casting in a four-jaw independent chuck.

We will first look at the three-jaw chuck. The best method of making a component in one of these is, if possible, to turn it completely at one set-up. If you put a piece of bar into the chuck, face the end, centre drill, drill and ream it, skim the diameter and part it off, it should be concentric all over. This is because we have turned it all at the same setting without taking it out of the chuck.

If we need to machine the other end, however, when we turn it round and put it back in the chuck, the chances are it will not run true.

This is where the four-jaw independent chuck comes in. You can put the component into a four-jaw chuck and set it to run true using the dial test indicator. Any work you do on the parted off end should then be concentric with the rest of the component. When setting work in a four-jaw independent chuck for a second operation, use some thin shim between the jaws and the workpiece to avoid marking the work.

Work is often held in a four-jaw chuck because it is a casting, an odd shape or square and so won't fit into a three-jaw chuck. If the work just requires to be faced flat right across the face, there is no need to set the work running radially true. It should be near enough on the centre line as long as the work is reasonably balanced.

You could, of course, put the component into a three-jaw chuck by fitting soft jaws and machining or boring them out to take the component. This is the best option if making several components that need to be identical, but if you only need one or two components a four-jaw independent chuck will be the quickest method of machining them.

Larger diameters can be held in a three-jaw chuck by using the outside jaws. These have a large radius on the inside of the jaw; if this radius is larger than the workpiece, the jaws should not tend to dig into the work and mark it. Outside jaws are useful for holding components like small flywheels, locomotive wheels and chuck backplates when machining the bores of holes or when machining across the face.

When machining thin discs, it is useful to put some packing behind the disc to make it stand proud of the jaws. To stop the packing flying out when the machine is running, make a set of three or four packing pieces with grooves at each end and fit tension springs to them. They should all be the same diameter so that the back of the work is parallel to the chuck. The length and grooves can vary slightly as they don't affect the parallelism. They are quick and simple to make, so a couple of sets of different diameters should find their way into everybody's toolbox.

## Chuck Keys

I have already mentioned that the chuck key should never be left in the chuck when it is unattended (see Chapter 2). Put the key into the chuck, use it and put it safely away as soon as you have finished with it. If you switch on the lathe with the key still in the chuck you might need a trip to the hospital.

Do not use excessive force when you tighten up the chuck. Do not use a piece of tube, a spanner or anything else as a lever; the chuck key on its own should be sufficient to tighten the chuck onto the work.

When using a four-jaw chuck, a small chuck key, little more than a knurled knob with a square on, can be used to adjust the jaws in and out prior to tightening up with the proper chuck key. This will save time over adjusting the jaws with a large chuck key.

To turn the independent four-jaw chuck jaws round, a carpenter's brace with a piece of square bar in it to fit the chuck will make short work of reversing the jaws, but don't use it for the final tightening as it is liable to strain the jaws.

## STARTING TO TURN

Before going any further, you need to learn how to do basic turning. For this you need to put the three-jaw chuck onto the mandrel. Start by cleaning the mandrel with a clean bit of rag or similar (I keep a roll of paper kitchen towelling in the workshop). Now you need to clean the chuck's bore and thread using the two toothbrush method (*see* Chapter 2). Both the mandrel and the chuck should be clean before you attempt to fit the chuck to the lathe.

Selecting and grinding turning tools has already been discussed (see Chapter 4), so by now you should have a correctly ground turning tool suitable for roughing out a piece of steel bar.

## Making a Tool Centre Height Setting Gauge

This tool needs its cutting edge set to the centre height of the lathe. There are several ways to do this but one of the easiest is with a home-made height gauge. When starting out, this is a chicken and egg situation: you need to make the gauge to set the height, but you also need a tool set at the correct height to make the gauge.

The simplest way to overcome this problem is to set the lathe tool to the approximate centre height and take a cut across the face of the bar. Depending on whether there is a pip remaining on the end of the bar, you should get an idea how far out the tool height is. If there is no pip this means the tool is on correct centre height or too high. A pip means the tool is too low. Of course you may have been lucky, so try dropping the tool slightly until a pip remains. You can then raise the tool a few thou at a time until

*Although most lathe chuck keys have square ends, they are often of different sizes. Keep each key with its own chuck.*

*Bar with a pip: tool above or below centre height.*

*Bar with no pip: tool on centre.*

using power feed if you have it and making sure you knock the feed off before it hits the chuck. Stop the lathe and wind the carriage to the start of the bar. Take another cut at the same setting and make a note of the diameter. Take another shallow cut, but this time go only about ¼in (6mm) along the bar, knock the feed off and turn the lathe off. Move the carriage towards the tailstock so that you can measure the bar. Continue making this cut and measure until the size is correct. Then run the tool along the full length of the job. Wind the carriage back towards the tailstock and take a finishing cut or two at the same setting. The diameter should now be the exact size required.

It is not difficult to turn accurately, it just takes a little patience and practice. The more turning you do, the easier you will find it is to hold accurate limits. If you turn everything accurately, whether it needs to be accurate or not, you will soon learn to turn within a thou or so without any problems.

Now we need to make a tool height setting gauge. Cut a length of bar just over the dimensions you wrote down and face one end, turn it round in the chuck and face the other end. Measure the length and find out how much you have to take off it

the pip disappears. The tool should then be on centre height.

Now that the tool is at centre height, you can make a simple height gauge. Turn a piece of bar down to as close to ½in (12mm) as you can get and leave it in the lathe chuck. Measure from the top of the cross slide to the top of the bar with a cheap height gauge.

Lower the height gauge by half the bar diameter. The height gauge should be exactly on the lathe centre line. Make a note of this dimension.

We now need to look at how to turn a bit of bar to an accurate diameter. When turning a bar to, say, ½in (12mm) you need to start with something slightly larger. In this case this will be ⁵⁄₈in (16mm) diameter material as this is a standard size.

Cut a piece of material about 2in (50mm) long and put it into the chuck with about 1in (25mm) sticking out. Skim the outside down to about 0.510 thou or 12.25mm, which is 10 thou (0.25mm) above the size required.

(You should be aware that most hobby lathe dials remove twice what they say: a one thou division, for example, will usually take 2 thou from the diameter. Larger commercial lathes are much more likely to take off one thou per graduation.)

Now take small cuts until almost to size,

*Measuring the height of the bar above the cross slide.*

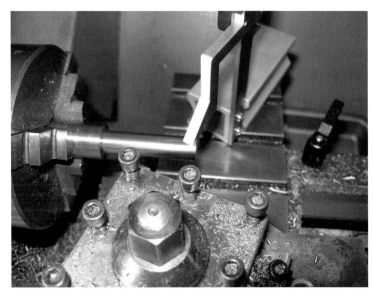

*Setting the height gauge to the lathe centre height.*

*Setting the height of the tool.*

*Using the setting gauge to set the height of the rear tool.*

to give the dimension you want. Put the bar back into the chuck and bring the tool up to the face of the bar. Lock the cross slide. Face the bar to length by using the top slide index, moving forwards a few thou at a time until the required length is reached. You now have a tool height setting gauge suitable for the front and rear tools.

If you have an inverted Vee bed lathe, or if for any reason you can't use the height gauge flat on the bed, you can put the height gauge on a plate on top of the lathe bed while you are setting the tool height.

## Turning to a Specific Length and Diameter

Now we will turn a bar with a step on the end. To ensure that the step is the correct length, we will use a bed stop. This can be as simple as a block clamped to the lathe bed to stop the carriage moving any further. I use a simple home-made bed stop that does all I require.

Set the bed stop, then move the carriage until it touches the stop and lock it. Wind the top slide so that the tool is just touching the end of the bar and lock the carriage. For this exercise, we will make the step 16mm long and 12mm in diameter. Wind the top slide along 15.9mm. We can now rough out the step at each end. Turn the end down to about 0.2mm above the finished diameter by winding the carriage back and forth. You can use the fine feed, but make sure you knock the feed off before the carriage reaches the stop and finish up to the stop by hand. Wind the top slide along the remaining 0.1mm to 12mm and finish the diameter to size and length, taking light cuts as previously. Don't forget to clean up the face of the shoulder you have just turned.

If you need to use a bed stop at the tailstock end of the lathe, a simple method of doing this is to use a bar placed on the lathe bed against the tailstock. The bar acts

*A home-made bed stop.*

as a stop when the carriage is wound back towards the tailstock. This tailstock end bed stop is useful when you are turning a groove in a component and you need stops set at both the headstock and tailstock ends of the lathe.

**Turning Work on the Outside of the Inside Jaws**

The outside of the inside (drill) jaws are useful for turning larger diameter work that is too large to fit inside the drill jaws. This will most often be in the form of a flywheel casting. Flywheels with six spokes are ideal for turning in a three-jaw chuck as the spokes can fit between the chuck jaws. Ideally you need to tighten up the flywheel until it is tight, but not so tight as to distort the rim.

*Turning a step on a bar using the stop. The bar is held in the three-jaw chuck and supported with the tailstock centre.*

*A useful tailstock end back stop method.*

To ensure concentricity you should do as much work as possible on the casting at the same time. You should be able to turn the outside rim of the casting, face the rim, face the boss and drill, bore and ream for the crankshaft all at the same setting. All you need to do then is to fit the outside jaws, reverse the casting in the chuck, tap it gently back onto the steps of the outside jaws and face across the second side of the rim and the hub. Use a bit of shim to protect the flywheel diameter. It does not matter if the flywheel runs exactly true or not as you are only facing it parallel and to width, not turning any diameters to size.

## Using the Soft Jaws

Soft jaws are very useful when a component has to run dead true in the jaws, for example when making something like a grinding spindle where concentricity is important.

*Holding a flywheel in a three-jaw chuck.*

Soft jaws likely to be found in the home workshop are simple rectangles of steel with the scroll and groove formed directly into the soft jaws. Another type of jaw you may come across has a grooved pattern in the main jaws that matches a similar pattern in the actual soft jaws. The soft tops of these jaws are usually interchangeable. They are more likely to be found on larger chucks, but you could make your own version for the smaller sizes of chuck if you wish.

The main use of soft jaws is for second operation work, for example when you have turned a component complete from a bit of bar and parted it off. Now you need to hold the component true to finish off the second end. You can do this by boring out the chuck jaws to the exact diameter of the workpiece.

To bore the soft jaws, they should be tightened in the same direction as they will be tightened in use, so that they are operating on the same part of the chuck scroll every time. If you have a thin component to machine, fit the soft jaws to the chuck and

*Holding a flywheel in the outside jaws.*

*Boring soft jaws to fit the work. The jaws are closed onto an oddment of bar to turn the shallow register so that it takes the work.*

clean the bore thoroughly before trying the workpiece, since loose dust can make the hole seem smaller than it really is. When the workpiece enters the bore, finish boring right through the jaws; go through a couple of times at the same setting to take out any spring in the boring bar. You can now remove the disc, clean the jaws and put the workpiece right through the chuck, checking that it runs dead true.

This operation may sound time consuming for a single item, but if you have several components to make it will save a considerable time on setting up each bar individually to run true.

Now the screws are in place we can work the other way round and hold components on the outside of the jaws. To do this, you will

tighten the jaws onto a bit of bar held in the chuck. Be sure to leave enough space in front of the bar so you can bore the jaws to fit the work.

Always use the same chuck key hole when tightening up the jaws. This applies to anything you do with a self-centring chuck. Stamp a cross or a centre pop mark against one of the jaws; I suggest doing this next to jaw No. 1, but any one will do as long as you always use the same marked hole. You might as well mark all your self-centring chucks in the same manner.

Carefully bore the jaws to the exact diameter of the work to be machined. Try to get it exactly on size. Undo the jaws slightly, remove the bar and replace it with the workpiece, which should now run dead true.

A useful modification to the soft jaws is to drill and tap a hole in the middle of the jaws and fit an Allen screw to each hole. If you want to hold a long bar in the soft jaws, it is now easy to bore all the way through the jaws rather than just boring a step or part way through. All you need to do now is find a disc of material to put into the chuck, ensuring there is sufficient material left on the inside edges of the chuck jaws to bore right through to take the bar.

Hold the disc on the screw heads; if necessary, drill the disc before boring. Bore right through the disc and the jaws until you

are nearly to size, at which point you can bore through the disc and test the resulting bore with the workpiece. Make sure you

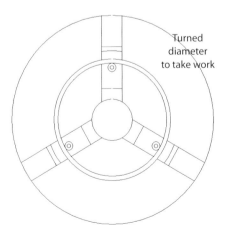

*Boring soft jaws using a ring. The soft jaws have three Allen screws that are closed down onto the ring while boring.*

*Turning the outside of the soft jaws using a ring. The soft jaws have three Allen screws that are opened up onto the ring while turning.*

need a ring of a suitable size onto which you can tighten the jaws with the jaw loading acting outwards, so any component you put on the outside of the jaws will be running concentrically. This will be ideal for items such as traction engine wheel rims and other large hollow or tubular workpieces.

One other use for soft jaws is to hold irregular-shaped components. Put a piece of bar into the soft jaws and bore a hole of any size, and then clean up the bore so that all of the jaws are true. Transfer the chuck to the milling machine table and clamp it down. Use a test indicator to check that the hole in the chuck is true.

You can now mill a nest to take any irregularly shaped component, confident that when the chuck is returned to the lathe it will be running true.

## Dial Test Indicators

There are two main types of dial test indica-

*Plunger type dial test indicator.*

*Lever type dial test indicator.*

tor: the plunger type dial test indicator, as its name suggests, works on a plunger principle, while the lever type dial test indicator has a stylus on the end. The lever stylus is usually ball- or pear-shaped and is fixed to the dial test indicator with a friction fit, meaning that it can be moved up and down on the end of the dial test indicator through a wide arc to put it into the best position for use.

The plunger type dial indicator usually has a maximum plunger movement of ½in (12mm), but plunger movements of up to 2in (50mm) are available. The plunger type dial indicator is non-reversing and needs an adaptor to enable it to clock holes true. Instead of a stylus it has an interchangeable end, often with a ball fitted; various interchangeable ends are available or you can make your own.

The lever dial test indicator has a much smaller range of travel: a range of 0.008in (0.2mm) is very common. It is usually either self-reversing (it moves when in contact with the work, depending on which way it is moving) or it may be reversed by using a lever on the side of the dial test indicator; both types are quite common. Since the stylus is delicate, combined with its limited travel range, you must be very careful not to break it.

A plunger dial indicator can be used as a direct readout of the travel and will be found to be very accurate. Owing to the relatively long travel, if you wanted perhaps to offset the centre of a bit of bar in the four-jaw chuck by 0.125in (3.18mm), this can

be done by turning the chuck by hand and setting the bar until the indicator travel shows 0.250in (6.35mm), which is 0.125in (3.18mm) offset. The lever dial test indicator is of no use for giving direct readings like this, but should be used as a comparator where the reading taken is, for example, zero at all points of the travel.

The dial test indicator is usually mounted on a magnetic or vacuum base, but is sometimes fixed to a block that can be clamped to the lathe, most often on the cross slide. Sometimes the dial test indicator comes as a complete kit including various mounting components.

## Four-jaw Chuck

To set the work up in an independent four-jaw chuck we first need to know what part of the workpiece should be on the centre. If the workpiece is a casting we may have an outside diameter, or a hole, that needs to run true; in this case we would put a dial test indicator onto the work and adjust the chuck a little at a time until the diameter runs true. Do not turn the chuck with

*Clocking the end of a casting in a four-jaw chuck.*

*Where a casting is sticking out, as here, you should try to support the casting with a running centre. This will help to stop the casting shifting in the chuck.*

the indicator in the hole. Instead, wind the carriage forwards until the clock enters the hole and take a reading. Wind the carriage back, rotate the chuck 90 degrees, wind the carriage forward and take another reading. Adjust the work in the chuck until it runs true.

### Lathe Centre Finder

If there is no diameter or hole, you may have to mark out the centre on the work using a

height gauge, and centre pop it with a centre punch. Then you can use a wobbler and a test indicator to set the work true.

It was once possible to get a lathe centre finder consisting of a bar about 6in (150mm) long, pointed at both ends, with a universal joint about 1in (25mm) from the front end. In use, the short front end goes in the centre pop of the work in the chuck. When you rotate the chuck by hand, the pointed short end follows the eccentricity of the centre hole, which is magnified about six

*A simple home-made centre finder.*

times at the tailstock end. You then just have to adjust the chuck until the tailstock end is running true, at which point the centre in the work will also be running dead true. I don't know anyone who makes these and second-hand ones are extremely rare.

You can make a simple version of this that works well by using a milling machine pointed centre finder. This is a parallel bar with a separate moveable pointed end. The two components are held together with a spring inside. You need the pointed edge finder, a Morse taper parallel adaptor (the Morse taper should fit your tailstock), a spring and a short stub of bar that will fit inside the tapered holder's bore to stop the spring going right through. Put the short stub of bar into the taper, insert the spring, follow up with the centre and put the Morse taper adaptor into the tailstock. Bring the tailstock towards the chuck until the centre of the centre finder is in the centre pop. The spring will hold it in place. To use the improvised

*Using a scribing block with a dial test indicator.*

centre finder, put a dial test indicator onto the parallel part of the centre finder's point and rotate the chuck by hand. The point will rotate eccentrically; adjust the chuck until the centre finder's point is running true.

Move the tailstock along the bed until the point of the wobbler is in the centre pop on the work. Put the test indicator on the front diameter of the wobbler and adjust the chuck jaws until the wobbler is running true.

When setting up a casting or something similar, where not all of the diameters are machined, you should use the dial test indicator on diameters that will not be machined, such as the inside of a flywheel rim. When you have turned all the finished diameters, they should then be true with the unmachined diameters.

Setting work in the four-jaw chuck depends on the component to be machined. If you are using round material, you can set it to run true using a dial test indicator. However, if you are setting a rough casting, the variation of size and roughness of the castings may well be unsuitable for a dial test indicator.

There are alternative methods of setting work up in a four-jaw chuck, especially for castings. One of the simplest methods is to hold a square bar in the lathe tool holder and use this to set the job true. In use, you wind the bar up to the work and set the dial to zero, or otherwise make a note of where it is. Wind the bar out or away from the work. Turn the chuck 180 degrees and wind the bar up against the work again. You can immediately see which way the bar needs to move so that it is running true. Adjust the casting in the four-jaw chuck and move the casting towards the centre point. Repeat until the casting is running true. This method is also useful if you are setting a square bar to run true. Just check each face of the square bar with the bit of metal.

*Setting a casting by using a square bar.*

## Sticky Pin Method

An alternative, the sticky pin method, is especially suited to locomotive wheels or flywheels. An ordinary household pin is mounted in plasticine or Blu-tack, perhaps stuck on the lathe tool, and is arranged to point to the inside diameter of the wheel or flywheel, the area that is not machined but is left as cast. Adjust the casting until the unmachined face is running as true as you can get it and the wheel is ready to turn. The sticky pin method is also useful for setting up work that has a chucking spigot, such as a locomotive smokebox door. Just hold the chucking spigot in the four-jaw chuck and adjust the casting until it runs true on the outside diameter and the front face.

The methods of centring work in the four-jaw chuck that have been discussed are also suitable for setting work true on the faceplate. The next chapter looks at turning between centres and using the faceplate.

*Using a commercial sticky pin to set work true.*

# 6    Turning between Centres and Faceplate Work

This chapter deals with basic turning between centres and then introduces turning with the work mounted on the lathe faceplate.

## TURNING PLAIN BARS BETWEEN CENTRES

The most basic way of holding work for turning is between centres. Turning between centres is literally holding the component to be machined between two centres, each of which has a 60-degree included angle. The headstock centre usually goes round with the headstock mandrel, although some older lathes had a non-rotating centre and the drive to the work was by a pulley mounted on the work. The tailstock centre is often a fixed centre that does not

*Tailstock plain centre.*

go round, although centres with ball bearings, called running centres, are readily available.

*Headstock centre and driver plate (also known as a catch plate).*

The component to be turned, usually a shaft, has a female 60-degree centre in both ends that is used to support the work. The work can be turned round between centres so that both ends of the shaft can be machined. Because the work is mounted between centres, both ends of the work will be true to each other.

### Centring the Bar

First, we have to put the centres into each end of the bar. If the bar is short, say up to about 6in long, hold the work in the three-jaw chuck and use a centre drill in the tailstock drill chuck to put a centre into the bar. A centre drill is a short drill with a small pilot on the end that has a 60-degree taper to the body diameter. A better method of centring the bar, especially long bars, is by using a three-jaw chuck and the fixed steady. The

*Tailstock running centre, so-called because it runs on ball races.*

Mark a line across the end of the bar with a scriber, turn the centre square 90 degrees and then scribe another line. Where the two lines cross is the centre of the bar. To make it easier to see the scribed lines, blacken the end of the bar with a permanent felt tip marker before scribing. Centre punch the point where the two lines cross and put a 60-degree centre in each end of the bar using a centre drill in a power drill. Hold the bar in a bench vice while doing this. Put a centre drill into the tailstock drill chuck and insert the bar in the three-jaw chuck. Make sure the lathe is on a low speed, about 300rpm, wind the tailstock in and just lightly clean up the centre hole with the centre drill to true it up.

Another useful tool to find the centre of a bar is a bell centre punch. This comprises a cone with a centre punch in the middle. In use, place the bell end on the end of the bar and tap the centre punch with a hammer to mark the centre. The end of the bar, though, needs to be reasonably square if using the bell punch method.

bar is held in the three-jaw chuck with the other end supported in the fixed steady and the centre is formed in the end with a centre drill.

A useful tool that can be used to find the centre of the shaft is the centre square, which is a metal blade with a Vee on it that locates on the diameter of the bar.

*Turning between centres.*

*Centring the bar using the fixed steady. (Note that the front clamp is normally done up while in use.)*

*A simple centre square.*

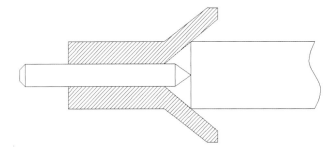

*Cross section of bell centre punch.*

There are other similar methods of centring bars but those given here will be all the turner needs to learn.

### Machining the Bar

Now we need to mount the bar between centres. This is simply a matter of putting the bar between centres and tightening the tailstock so it is lightly pressing into the centre in the end of the work. To drive the work, a carrier is fixed to the shaft and engages a pin in a catch plate mounted on the lathe mandrel. A catchplate is simply a blank disc with a pin sticking out to drive the carrier that is fitted to the work. The carrier is fitted to the work using an Allen screw or bolt. To stop any movement of the bar in relation to the catch plate, the carrier can be wired to the catchplate pin. This will stop the carrier and the work flapping about. It is

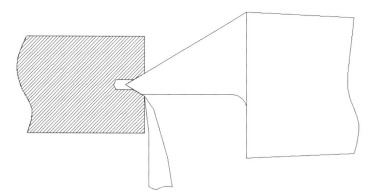

*Facing off a bar using the half centre.*

the end of the work without touching the half centre.

When using any fixed centre in the tailstock, put a bit of oil or grease into the centre before use and top up as necessary. Lightly wind the tailstock barrel against the centre and lock the barrel so it can't move. Switch the lathe on and wind the tool across to clean up the end. Reverse the work and clean the other end up at the same setting. Both centres should now be the same depth. Measure the overall length of the bar. Take the finished length required from the overall measurement you have just measured. Divide this by two and this is how much we need to take off each end of the shaft so it finishes at the required length.

If you have one, change the tailstock half centre to a running centre; if you don't have a running centre, change to a fixed centre. The half centre should only be used when facing the end of the bar. We will now machine the rest of the bar. For the purpose

particularly important to stop the work from moving in relation to the catchplate when screwcutting between centres.

Now that the bar is safely mounted between centres, we can start turning it to size. Normally the first thing to do is to face the ends of the bar to the finished length. Decide which end of the bar has the shallower centre. We will machine this end first. You will need a half centre, so-called because almost half of the centre is missing. This means the lathe tool can reach right across

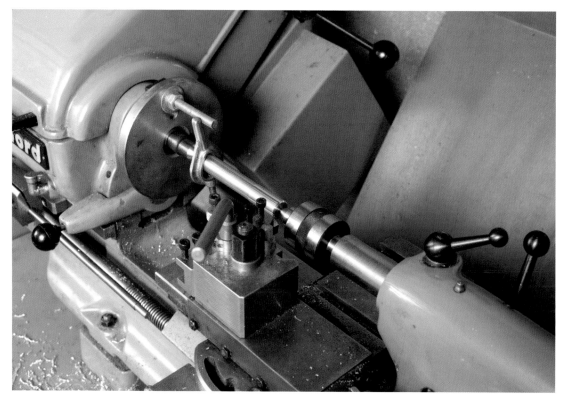

*A skimmed bar.*

of this example, we will assume the bar has a finished diameter in the middle with a step at each end. First we will machine the overall diameter to size. To do this, we need to skim the diameter and check the size. Take a fine cut along the bar, using the fine feed if you have one. Measure both ends of the bar. If you have set the lathe up correctly (see Chapter 2), the bar should be parallel. If it is not, adjust the tailstock before continuing. Assuming the bar is parallel, take another cut or two so that you are about 0.1mm larger than the finished diameter. Now move the tool in until almost at finished size and take a light cut about 10mm long along the bar. Repeat this cut to ensure the tool is not pushing off. Measure this diameter; you will probably have to wind the tailstock barrel back to get the micrometer onto the end of the bar. Only move the barrel back, do not slide the entire tailstock back. Measure the bar to find out how much to remove from the diameter. Take another short cut and check for size. When the bar is cutting to size, machine all the way along. You will probably have to take two or three cuts at the same setting until the bar is machined to finished size.

Now we will turn the steps on the ends. To ensure that the steps are the correct length, we will use the bed stop. Set the bed stop, then wind the top slide so that the tool is just touching the end of the bar. For this exercise we will make the steps 12mm long. Wind the top slide along until the tool is just touching the end of the turned bar. Wind the top slide along 11.9mm. We can now rough out the step at each end. Turn the end down to about 0.2mm above the finished diameter. You can use the fine feed but make sure you knock the feed off before the carriage reaches the stop and finish up to the end by hand. Repeat for the other end. Wind the top slide along the remaining 0.1mm to 12mm and finish each end in the same way as you finished the main diameter. Don't forget to clean up the face of the shoulder you have just turned.

Congratulations, you have just turned an accurate shaft. Don't worry if the shaft is a tiny bit undersize, you can probably make the mating holes to fit.

*The finished shaft.*

Using the method set out above, you should now be able to turn any shaft you require within the capacity of the lathe. A variation of the above method, where the shaft is single-ended, is to hold one end in the three- or four-jaw chuck and support the other end with a centre in the tailstock.

*Using a chuck and a running centre.*

*A large faceplate; smaller ones are available.*

## FACEPLATE WORK

Another basic way of holding work is on the faceplate. This method is used when the component is too large or is awkwardly shaped and would be difficult to hold in a three- or four-jaw chuck. Usually the work is clamped directly onto the faceplate, often with a packing piece behind it to protect the faceplate.

The faceplate should be flat and true, so the first thing to do when you get the lathe is to check the faceplate with a dial test indicator. Carefully clean the mandrel nose and the internal hole in the faceplate. Make sure the mandrel can turn freely by hand with the lathe switched off and check that the face of the faceplate is running true as close to the outer edge as you can get. If it is running true, run the test indicator across the front face of the faceplate; this should be true as well. If the faceplate is running out, it will need to be machined. Put the lathe into back gear if it has it (top back gear

will probably be fine). You will need a carbide-tipped tool, ideally with a small 45-degree chamfer on the tip. Bring the tool up to the faceplate and lock the carriage. Next you need to lightly face the faceplate right across its diameter. If you have a power cross feed it will make light work of this, but if not you can feed across by hand. Fortunately most faceplates have a series of rings on them to aid in setting up the work. Machine the faceplate from the outside to the first ring and stop for a rest, feed to the second ring and so on until finished. Depending upon how badly out your faceplate is, you may have to do this more than once until it is cleaned up, but when it is done you will rarely need to do this exercise again.

### Machining a hole in a block

As mentioned previously, the rings machined on the faceplate are guides to help you set up the work. This will do if the work is a

round component, but we need a different method if the work is square. Take a block of metal, for example, that has been machined all over. We want to machine a hole in it 2in from one edge and 1in from another edge. Mark out the position of the hole and centre punch it. Put a dead centre into the tailstock, hold the block onto the faceplate, bring the tailstock up towards the chuck and lock it. Wind the tailstock barrel and centre up to the component and engage with the centre pop. Lock the tailstock barrel. Clamp the block to the faceplate using some packing pieces and four clamps on the block. The hole is now on centre and we can machine it in the correct place.

If we need more than one hole placed accurately in the component we can use toolmaker's buttons to ensure the holes are in the correct place. Toolmaker's buttons usually come in sets of four. One button is usually longer than the rest so you can still clock the diameter when it is close to another hole. Sets are often avail-

*Setting up the faceplate using the tailstock.*

able second-hand on eBay; while they probably have an obscure American thread, you can clamp them to the block using your own BA or metric screws, together with a washer.

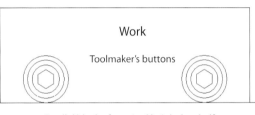

*A set of toolmaker's buttons.*

To fit them to the component to be bored, mark out, drill and tap holes in the approximate positions where the holes are needed. If you need a pair of parallel holes, place the

component on a surface plate, loosely fit the buttons and push them down onto a parallel or similar block of the correct thickness and nip the screws up. The spacer should be smaller than required by half the diameter of a button.

If the holes need to be a certain distance apart, use a spacer of the correct size between the buttons. (Remember to make the spacer smaller by one diameter of the button.)

*Setting up a component using toolmaker's buttons to get a fixed distance from the edge of a component.*

There are lots of different ways to set the spacing of buttons. It is mainly a matter of common sense.

Castings and flat components can be bolted to the faceplate for machining. A typical example of a flat component is an eccentric strap. This type of component is usually made of a component that is cut in half and bolted back together. A hole is then bored in it, on the centre line, to fit the eccentric. This type of component is often

Work

Toolmaker's buttons

Parallel block of required height less half diameter of toolmaker's button

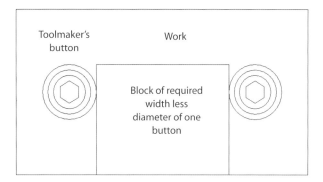

*Setting up a component using toolmaker's buttons to get a fixed distance between the centres of a component.*

difficult to hold in the lathe chuck and is prone to distortion. Castings are often too large to fit into a lathe chuck and so the faceplate is called on to undertake the work. A casting can often be bolted directly to the faceplate to facilitate easy machining.

Work on the faceplate is often an odd shape or is set off centre. This causes it to be unbalanced and as a consequence the lathe may vibrate while the work is turning. To counteract this tendency, the faceplate should be counterbalanced by bolting weights onto it. A useful source of weights is the lathe's change wheels. By bolting a change wheel or two onto the lighter side of the faceplate, you can bring the whole assembly back into balance. After bolting the change wheels on, spin the lathe by hand to check the balance. The faceplate should not show a tendency to stop at one particular point. When you are happy that

the faceplate is in balance, the work and balance weights are bolted on tightly, and so that the work does not foul the lathe when turned by hand, switch the machine on in low back gear to check for vibration. Depending on what you are turning, you should be able to run in top back gear or even bottom direct speed.

**Turning a Flywheel**

One of the main uses of a faceplate is turning a large diameter iron casting, typically a flywheel or a locomotive wheel for a steam engine. The flywheel should be mounted so

that the inner edge of the rim and the outer edge of the hub run true. If either of them runs out, it would be better that the hub runs out as the rim will be more noticeable on the finished engine.

Clamp the flywheel down with some packing under the spokes so that you can turn right across the rim. Be careful that you clamp the flywheel tight enough so that it does not move, but not so tight that it distorts.

Rough turn the outside diameter and face the rim using the back gear. Using a direct drive speed, drill and bore the centre hole, and either finish off with the boring tool or use a ream. Don't try reaming without boring; the chances are that if you do, the hole will not be true with the rim as the drill probably did not cut an accurate hole. Drop down to the top back gear speed; face the rim and turn the outside of the rim to the finished diameter. Turn the flywheel over and finish the other face to width.

**Turning Locomotive Wheel Flanges**

Locomotive wheel flanges can be turned on a faceplate. You can purchase blank end Morse taper arbors that fit into the headstock taper. Fit one of these and turn a

*A simple clamp set is very useful when machining a casting on the faceplate.*

*A stub arbor suitable for centralizing a locomotive wheel or flywheel.*

*Using the Keats Vee angle plate to turn an eccentric component.*

spigot on it to take the wheel bore. The wheel bores should all be the same size, but if they are different sizes machine the spigot to fit the largest bore, machine the flange on that one, then machine the spigot down to fit the next one, machine the flange and so on.

Ideally the wheel bores should all be the same size, but if they are not, proceed as follows. Skim the outside diameter of the wheel flange, measure and take it to the correct finished size. Move the lathe tool in by the depth of the flange and turn the tread. Deal with all wheels like this, machining all of the flange outside diameters to the same size, moving in the cross slide by the same amount each time so that all the treads end up the same size.

## Keats Vee Angle Plate

The Keats Vee angle plate is mounted on the faceplate and is used to hold round bar, square bar and miscellaneous castings such as cylinders and steam chests. The angle plate can be mounted anywhere on the faceplate as long as the lathe can be rotated safely and is in balance. When spun by hand, the faceplate should not show a tendency to stop at any particular place; when run under power, the lathe should not vibrate.

As well as holding bar and castings for turning, the Keats Vee angle plate is very useful for making eccentric components such as the eccentrics for a steam engine.

To turn an eccentric, use a test indicator to check that the round bar is running reason-

ably true. When this is satisfactory, you can turn the outside diameter of the bar to fit the eccentric strap (or component), including any step or groove required. Next, offset the Keats Vee angle plate by the amount you want the eccentric 'throw' to be. Use the dial test indicator to measure the offset of the outside of the eccentric. The offset should be twice the throw. You can now drill, bore and ream the hole in the eccentric.

You now have enough basic knowledge to carry out turning between centres and work accurately on the faceplate. In the next chapter we will look at holding work in a collet and on a mandrel.

# 7 Collets and Mandrels

This chapter explains all about holding work in a collet, and how you can make and use several different types of mandrel for workholding.

## USING COLLETS

Quite a few different collet systems are to be found in workshops. Some are used for holding tools such as milling cutters, some are used for bar or workpieces, while some may be used with both bar and workpieces.

One of the commonest is the ER collet, which comes in several different sizes, each having a different large diameter. The ER collet system allows up to 0.039in (1mm) collapse of a collet, although in the smaller sizes you can buy the collets in 0.5mm increments. A 16mm collet, for example, will hold round material down to 15mm diameter. Whatever the ER collet size, they all appear to go down to 1mm minimum, which will close down to 0.5mm.

There are many types and sizes of ER

holder available. All the usual Morse taper shank sizes are available and you can also buy various diameters of extended paral-

ER collet adaptor.

lel shank holders. The problem with these is that they are great for holding tools that have a short shank, but because you need to use the holder with a drawbar, you can't put long bar stock right through them. To overcome this, for lathe work you can also buy ER collet holders designed to be fitted to a chuck backplate that you can machine to suit your lathe, so ensuring good concentricity. Because they don't use a drawbar, you can fit bar stock right through and into the headstock mandrel.

When buying new and second-hand ER collets make sure they have the retaining groove near the nose end. The older (and obsolete) E and ES collet types do not have the retaining groove and are not inter-

ER collets.

ER collet adaptor fitted to a backplate. I always leave backplates oversize so I have something with which to clamp them down when used on a mill or drill.

changeable. You are most likely to find E and ES collets included with a second-hand Unimat lathe.

Draw-in collets are used with a drawbar or collet tube. The drawbar draws the collet up tight by drawing it into the lathe's mandrel by a bar that runs through the centre of the mandrel and screws into the centre of the collet. This means that you cannot put bar stock right through the collet. To overcome this, some Morse taper collets use a hollow draw tube, the collet having an external thread to match the internal thread of the draw tube.

*Draw-in collet.*

Special collets are made for the Myford ML7, Super 7 and ML10 lathes. These are Morse taper collets but, rather than having a drawbar, they are closed with a nose ring that fits over a groove in the collet. The nose ring tightens the collet into the headstock mandrel's Morse taper. It is

extracted after use by undoing the nose piece, which draws the collet out from the Morse taper by the nose groove. Imperial and metric collets are available up to ½in (12mm) diameter.

Dead length collets are available that fit into an attachment usually fixed to the front of the lathe's mandrel. These collets are called dead length because they do not move longitudinally, unlike draw-in collets. You are more likely to find collets like these second-hand rather than new.

*Dead length collet.*

A variation of the dead length collet is the Crawford Multibore collet. This system has

collets made of segments held together by springs. The collets are of variable diameter and have quite a large closure range. They are more likely to be found on a larger commercial lathe, although you can get collets for smaller machines.

Watchmaker's collets can be used in most lathes by making an adaptor for the headstock and a drawbar (or tube). Watchmaker's collets are very accurate and can go down to very small sizes, but they have limited use in most workshops. You can get a special watchmaker's spindle for the Emco Unimat lathe and there is also a version of the Cowells lathe, the CW90, that takes watchmaker's collets.

For most of the work carried out on the lathe, you will find that an ER holder that mounts onto a chuck backplate is most useful.

## MAKING MANDRELS

There are several types of mandrel in common use in workshops. The most common is probably the expanding mandrel, which can easily be made in any workshop. In its most basic form, it is a bar turned to a size to fit the bore in the workpiece. It is then threaded with a tapered tap and slit at 90 degrees to give four segments, which are then expanded by a screw fitted into the end of the mandrel.

*Boxed set of Myford collets.*

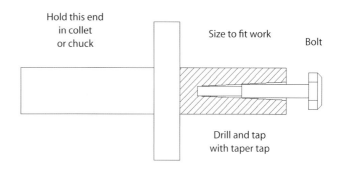

*Simple expanding mandrel.*

*Simple plain mandrel.*

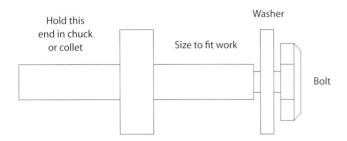

Hold this end in chuck or collet

Size to fit work

Washer

Bolt

Another common mandrel is the tapered mandrel. This is usually a 'between centres' mandrel and is often made to taper from just a couple of thou over nominal size to a couple of thou under nominal size. It is usually hardened and has a ground finish. The workpiece is held in place by being pushed onto the mandrel until it is tight. To remove it, just press it back out the way it went in.

Where concentricity is not quite so important, the workpiece can be put on a plain turned mandrel and tightened up with a bolt and flat washer.

Expanding mandrels are also made commercially, but as you need a mandrel for each individual size of hole it can get expensive if you need more than one or two different sizes. Commercial mandrels

can be obtained with Morse taper shanks to plug straight into the headstock. This method ensures that the mandrel should run dead true, assuming both the Morse taper mandrel and the Morse taper in the headstock are both clean and free from marks or swarf.

You can also purchase Morse taper arbors with blank end pieces from which to make your own mandrels. First we will make an expanding mandrel from a blank Morse taper arbor. You will need to turn the arbor down to fit the workpiece bore; I usually turn the mandrel about 0.010in (0.025mm) oversize to start with and then I drill and tap the arbor with a tapered tap. The drilled hole can go quite deep, but the tapped hole only needs to go in until the locking bolt is about halfway

down the length where the workpiece will sit.

Put the mandrel into the vice and cut along the mandrel, making four cuts around the circumference. Retap the hole to clear the swarf from the thread and put the mandrel back into the headstock taper. Now you can lightly nip the screw up to expand the mandrel slightly. Skim the mandrel to finished size until the workpiece will fit on without shake. You can now further tighten the screw so that the workpiece tightens onto the mandrel. When you slacken the screw the workpiece will come off easily, as you have skimmed it while it was slightly expanded. You can make an expanding mandrel from a bar held in the three- or four-jaw chuck, or perhaps a collet, in a similar way. If held in a chuck it may not go back true if you need to use it again, so if possible you should hold the arbor in a collet.

For a plain mandrel, turn the diameter to fit the workpiece, and drill and tap for a cap screw or a bolt. There is no need to split this type of mandrel. You simply put the workpiece onto the mandrel and hold it on with a flat washer. Again, it does not matter whether you use a bar in a chuck or collet, or if you use a Morse Taper blank arbor. Arbors are very useful in the workshop. If you make them from Morse taper blanks or hold them in a collet, they can be used over and over again.

# 8　Taper Turning and Lathe Accessories

This chapter explains how you can turn a taper using a top slide, the use of fixed and travelling steadies and form tools.

## TAPER TURNING

Sometimes you will have to turn a taper in the workshop. That is a fairly easy job. What is more difficult, however, is having to turn matching male and female tapers.

The method you are most likely to use in the workshop is to turn the two tapers with the top slide. You should be able to turn a taper long enough for a Morse taper using this method. The most important thing when turning tapers is to ensure that the tool tip is at the exact centre height of the lathe. This is because the taper will vary if the tool is not dead-on centre height.

Probably the easiest method of turning a Morse taper is to use a dial test indicator to clock a lathe centre of the required Morse taper between centres. The smaller end of the taper should be at the tailstock end of the lathe. The topslide should be wound along the taper by its handwheel, while the carriage remains locked. The topslide should be adjusted angularly until the dial test indicator reads zero all the way along.

Now you can finish turn the external Morse taper using an internal Morse taper sleeve as a gauge to check that the angle is correct. To do this, make marks with a felt tipped pen along the taper and check that the test sleeve rubs evenly all the way along the male taper. Adjust if necessary until you have a perfect fit.

To turn the matching female taper, the large end of the taper will be at the tailstock end and the boring bar will be inverted and cutting on the back of the hole. Doing this means that as long as both of the tools are at centre height, the tapers should match. We can use the male taper that has just been turned as a test bar. Bore out the taper very carefully; you won't need to remove much material before the test taper goes too far into the finished bore. Test with a felt tipped pen until you have a perfect fit.

You can turn any taper you need this way; you are not restricted to Morse tapers. Another method most often used for long, shallow tapers is to use a taper turning attachment. These attachments are often available as extras on higher quality lathes. They comprise a slide mounted onto the back of the lathe. Often the guide is dovetailed, with a sliding block attached to the cross slide to guide the tool on a taper. The depth of cut is usually put on using the top slide since the cross slide is usually discon-

*Turning a taper with the topslide.*

*Setting the top slide by clocking an existing taper.*

of the lathe the diameter will be larger at the tailstock end; if the tailstock is moved to the front, the tailstock end will be smaller in diameter. The amount of taper that can be turned in this manner is limited since the headstock and tailstock centres are out of line.

The final method of offsetting the workpiece is by using a boring head in the tailstock. You need a home-made hardened solid centre that fits where the boring tool would normally go. (A small Unimat lathe size running centre might be ideal.) Set the boring head so the tool travel is horizontal. You can then offset the boring head centre, so creating a taper. This is the same as setting the tailstock over but you don't have to realign the tailstock afterwards.

## USING FIXED AND TRAVELLING STEADIES

The fixed steady is used mainly to turn the end of a bar or to centre a workpiece that is too large to fit through the chuck. Obviously bar stock should not protrude from

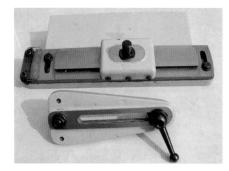
*Taper turning attachment.*

nected from the feed screw. In this way it is free to move in and out controlled by the guide.

Another method we shall look at for taper turning is to offset the tailstock on its base. This will make the work turned between centres become tapered, either large or small at the tailstock end depending on which way the tailstock is offset: if set towards the back

*Using the fixed steady.*

*The steady can be set using a chuck mounted on this tailstock adaptor.*

*Travelling steady.*

the chuck more than is necessary to work on. This is where the fixed steady comes in. The fixed steady can be set to the diameter of the bar so that the end of the bar can be machined safely.

One way to set the fixed steady to size is to turn a bit of bar in the chuck to the same size as the bar we want to use the steady on. Then we can move the fixed steady along the lathe bed and fit the workpiece into the chuck and in the steady. The end of the bar nearest to the tailstock should now be running true and can be worked on safely. The bar can be centre drilled, faced or otherwise worked on.

An alternative way to set the steady is to support the tailstock end of the bar with a three-jaw chuck mounted in the tailstock. Adaptors to take the three-jaw chuck are available or you could make your own. Just

*Setting the steady by using a chuck mounted on an adaptor.*

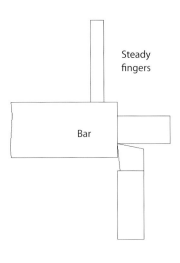

*Travelling steady with leading fingers.*

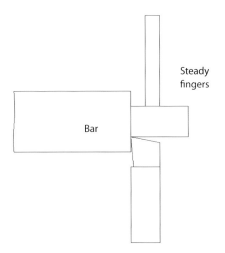

*Travelling steady with trailing fingers.*

support the bar at both ends in the three-jaw chucks and set the steady fingers to the bar.

The fixed steady can also be used to support tubes that do not have any material in the centre.

The fingers of the steady need to be lubricated regularly while in use. This is easily done by drilling a small hole in the top finger with a countersink inside the slot to take oil.

The travelling steady is most often used when turning down small diameter bars or screwcutting long slender bars. It bolts onto the front of the cross slide in line with the chuck and travels along when the cross slide is moved along the lathe bed. When turning, the travelling steady can either be set to the diameter of the bar before turning and to lead the tool or it can be set to the finished diameter required and to follow the tool. Normally the fingers are set to lead the turning tool, but if the bar is rough, for example if it is dented or rusty, it is better for the fingers to trail the turning tool. If screwcutting, the travelling steady should lead the tool so that it does not deflect or wear due to a burr being thrown up by the screwcutting tool.

Steadies will not be used very often but they are indispensable on the occasions when they are needed.

## MAKING A SIMPLE FORM TOOL

You may often need to produce a particular shape, such as a radius, on a component. The easiest method to do this is with a form tool. As an example, we will make a simple form tool to cut a half circle on a bar of brass. For a radius of 3mm, for example, we need to produce a form tool using a 6mm diameter drill or ream. For material we will use gauge plate, a high carbon steel that comes in the form of a ground flat bar. A piece about 5mm thick and 10mm wide is needed, although the size is not that important as long as the gauge plate is thick enough to absorb any turning stresses. Ideally we need a tapered reamer that will produce a 6mm diameter hole somewhere along its length, although you could use a parallel 6mm reamer, a slot drill or end mill, or even a standard twist drill.

Drill a hole through the gauge plate and open up to 6mm diameter. Aim to get a good surface finish on the sides of the hole. Hacksaw and file half the hole away to leave the shape required on the finish turned component. Now we need to harden the tool, although if we are just doing a component or two in brass we could probably get away without hardening it.

Hardening is simple enough: heat the working end of the tool to red, stop heating and let the gauge plate rest for a couple of minutes. This will give the gauge plate a chance to change its internal structure. Reheat to red and quench in a tub of water. This should harden the tool. Although a bit brittle, it should be fine for making a few components. Stone the top of the tool until the cutting edge is sharp. If necessary you can polish the inside of the radius that is going to do the cutting. There are several methods you can use, including a piece of wet and dry paper around a bit of bar, a very small grinding wheel called a mounted point, or a bit of round bar with fine valve grinding compound on it. Whichever you use, aim for a polished finish as the finish on the turned component is directly related to the finish on the form tool. You can make all sorts of simple form tools with gauge plate, a typical example being a facing tool with a 30-degree chamfer to face and chamfer nuts.

## Machining from a Template

You can machine a profile from a simple template. The template can be cut from gauge plate with a file or machined, but it does not need to be hardened. The template could be used to machine a large radius, such as a smokebox door. In use, the template is mounted on a block on the lathe bed and the cross slide is kept in contact with the template by being pushed against the template with a ball race fixed to the cross slide.

In the next chapter we will be looking at drilling and reaming.

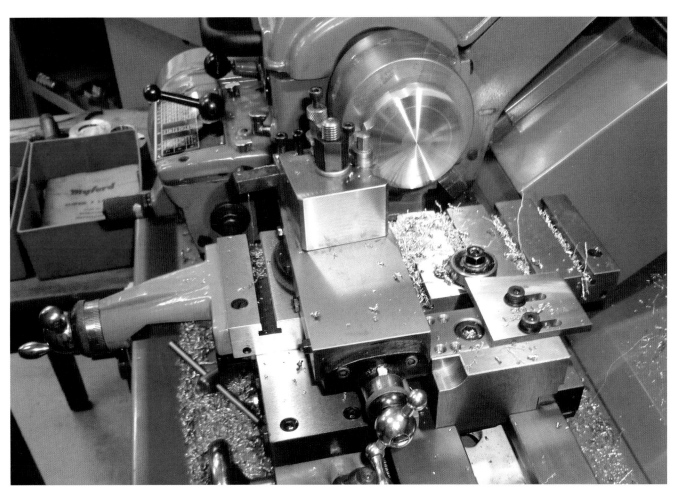

Copy template ready to use.

# 9  Drilling and Reaming

This chapter explains how to use drills and reamers in the lathe. There are many different types of drills and reamers. They are essential to making components in the lathe. We will look at the various types and how to choose the speeds and feeds for using them.

## TYPES OF DRILL

Drills are normally held either in the tailstock, if they have a Morse taper, or in a drill chuck if they have a parallel shank. A drill chuck is mounted on a Morse taper shank that is usually the largest Morse taper that

the tailstock will take. The largest size of drill that will normally fit a drill chuck is ½in (13mm) in diameter, although larger chucks are available at a cost. The smallest size of drill that a ½in (13mm) drill chuck will take is usually about $^{1}/_{16}$in (1.5mm). This is because the larger drill chuck is incapable of closing down enough to take the smaller sizes of drill. This means we will probably need two drill chucks, one for larger drills and one for smaller drills.

There are two main types of drill chuck. One is tightened by using a chuck key, which has a small bevel gear built on to it that mates with the outer sleeve of the drill

*Hand-tightening drill chuck.*

*This drill chuck requires a chuck key.*

chuck itself. The other type is hand tightened where the outer chuck sleeve is knurled; to tighten the drill the sleeve is turned by hand.

Larger drills above ½in (13mm) usually have a No. 1 or No. 2 Morse taper shank. You can get Morse taper sleeves to convert a large Morse to a smaller Morse taper. You can also get a small Morse to large Morse taper converter as well.

*Drill with a tapered shank.*

into model engineering, a set of number drills from No. 1 to No. 60 is to be recommended.

Drills are also available in different lengths. Stub drills are shorter than standard jobber drills. Several lengths of long series drills are also available, ranging from one and a half times the length of a jobber drill up to several times the length.

*Three-flute core drill.*

Some larger drills are also available with parallel shanks. They are made with a stepped down ½in parallel shank and are called blacksmith's drills.

*Different lengths of drills.*

*Blacksmith's drill.*

The most useful drills in the workshop come as sets of high speed steel jobber drills in a case. The most popular set covers 1mm to 6mm, increasing by 0.1 mm steps. Another useful set covers from 6mm to 10mm, also increasing by 0.1 mm steps. If you are

Most drills have two flutes, but core drills are also to be had with three, four or even more flutes. As their name suggests, these are usually used for drilling out cored holes in castings. Core drills are not normally capable of starting a new hole but are used for opening up existing holes.

A standard drill usually has an included angle of 118 degrees. Stub drills and cobalt drills often have a 135 to 140 degree angle for use on harder materials, such as stainless steel and aircraft steels.

Back rake on drills is often ground radially. Another type of point, however, has four facets to the point. Four-facet drills are much better at starting a hole than a standard jobber drill, which tends to wander unless following a centre pop or centre drill. Four-facet drills also require less pressure to drill a hole, since the point is thinner than a stand-

ard drill, and they are far easier to sharpen accurately by hand than standard jobber drills. Dormer do a range of four-facet drills, called A002, with a titanium nitride coating (TiN) and a four-facet point.

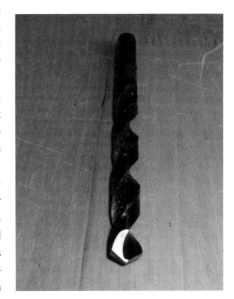
*Dormer A002 four-facet drill point.*

*A set of metric drills covering 1–6mm.*

To drill an accurate sized hole requires two or more steps: first you drill the hole

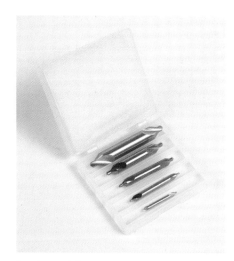

*Set of centre drills.*

the shank is the same size as the reamer, the middle is smaller (waisted) and the cutting end is the hole size. You can also get adjustable reamers, where the end is expanded by the use of a screw in the cutting end of the reamer.

*Hand reamer; the front part has a slight taper.*

*Waisted shank machine reamer.*

*Morse taper shank machine reamer.*

undersize (by perhaps ½mm), then you follow through with a size drill. The chances are the second drill will cut dead to size as it is only cutting a small amount from the diameter. Obviously, if you are drilling a large hole, more intermediate steps may be required. Speeds for drilling are the same as those given for turning in the table in Chapter 3.

## REAMERS

There are several types of reamers available for use in workshops, again with either Morse taper or parallel shanks. Some have size parallel shanks, the shank being the same size as the reamer, while others are available with shanks smaller than the reamed size. There is also the waisted reamer, where

*Straight shank machine reamer.*

Parallel reamers are divided into two types: parallel machine reamers, where the cutting diameter is the same all along the ream, and hand reamers, where the cutting end is slightly smaller and tapers up to the full diameter.

When drilling a hole for reaming it is advisable to use the two-hole method for

drilling. You are more likely to get a good size hole prior to reaming. For small reamers up to 0.4in (10mm), leave about 0.012in (0.3mm) for the reamer to remove. For reamers up to ¾in (19mm), leave 0.016in (0.4mm) and over ½in (13mm) leave 0.020in (0.5mm) For reaming speeds use about a third to a half of the drilling speed for the same diameter. Feeds should be from 0.002 to 0.004in (0.025–0.05mm) per tooth per rev. Multiply the feed per tooth by the number of teeth to give the feed per revolution.

It is best to use neat cutting oil for most materials except for aluminium, for which paraffin should be used, and plastic, which requires compressed air or plain water. You should not use oil as a cutting lubricant for any type of plastic as it can attack and/or degrade the plastic.

# 10 Boring Tools and Boring Heads

This chapter shows you how to bore holes in the lathe with the work held in a chuck, mounted on the faceplate or fixed to the lathe cross slide.

## DIFFERENT TYPES OF BORING BARS

Boring a hole to size is one of the most exacting jobs you can do in a lathe. It is relatively easy to turn a shaft to fit a hole, but it is much harder to bore an accurate hole to fit a shaft. If possible, you should bore the hole before turning the shaft.

You are likely to come across HSS boring bars or inserted tip boring bars. Both have their uses. The HSS tool is ideal for most general hole-boring jobs, but the inserted tip tool is far superior for materials such as cast iron. The boring bar should be as large as you can get into the hole while still allowing swarf to be removed.

The boring bar should only protrude far enough to enable it to go completely through the bore. Any more protrusion than is necessary may result in chatter, or a dig in, in the bore. The front clearance on the boring bar tip should be as small as possible without rubbing as strength is important.

Boring can be used to finish a hole to size or simply to true a hole up after drilling and prior to reaming. It is best to run the boring tool through the hole using a fine feed to the carriage if you have the feed option on your lathe. The final finishing cut should be put through two or three times at the same setting to eliminate any spring in the tool, work or lathe. If the hole has an intermittent cut through it, such as a cross hole, the hole is best bored to size.

It is possible to bore quite small holes if you have the right tool. Commercial 'small hole' boring tools are very expensive but I buy them second-hand whenever I see them, so I usually have a stock. It is easy, if time consuming, to grind up small boring bars but they are very useful especially when you need to true up a small hole prior to tapping or reaming.

End mills and slot drills make useful boring tools. As long as you get the cutting edge on centre height, they will bore as well as a proper boring bar, especially in aluminium.

You can make simple home-made boring tools by drilling and reaming a hole to take a HSS tool bit into a steel shank. Ideally the shank should be made of high tensile material or silver steel. The tool bit should be secured with a high tensile socket-headed grub screw or similar. The tool bit can either protrude from the side of the boring bar for through holes or protrude at the front of the shank at 45 degrees, if you are boring a blind hole.

*Typical HSS boring bar.*

Round boring bars can either be clamped into the Vee groove found in some toolholders or held in a split square shank. Either method is suitable, especially as the shank can be slid in or out of the tool holder to minimize protrusion.

Specially shaped tool bits can be used to undercut the end of the bore when it needs to be screwcut and can't be cut right through. Inserted HSS boring bars can also be ground up for undercutting before screwcutting.

There are several methods of checking a bore for accuracy. If you have to bore the hole to fit an existing component, perhaps a ballrace, you can use the existing component as a gauge or turn up a gauge. Rough out the bore within a few thou of the finished size, taking two or three spring cuts. Use a telescopic gauge, a pair of callipers with a micrometer or a digital vernier to measure the hole. Bore the start of the hole by no more than one thou at a time; do not go right through the bore. Test the front

of the bore: if the gauge does not go into the bore, run the tool right through under power feed. Bore out the front of the hole by another thou, check the bore and repeat until the gauge just goes into the start of the hole. Finish the bore at the same setting, checking that the gauge just enters. Take a couple of spring cuts to ensure the bore is parallel. You should now have an accurately sized hole.

The trick to boring is to finish with very fine cuts. Many engineers do not recommend fine cuts, but I have never had a problem as long as the tool is sharp.

## USING A BORING HEAD IN THE LATHE

Another method of boring a component in the lathe is to bolt it down to the cross slide. When the workpiece is bolted down and the hole position is lined up with the headstock, you can bore the hole in the workpiece in several ways.

First, however, you might need to put a

hole into the workpiece to clear the centre of the hole out of the way. You can do this by using a drill in a three- or four-jaw chuck (smaller drills could be used in a drill chuck). Start with a small drill and work up almost to the finished size of the hole to be bored.

*Checking a bore with a home-made gauge. The lead in is one thou smaller than the bore required.*

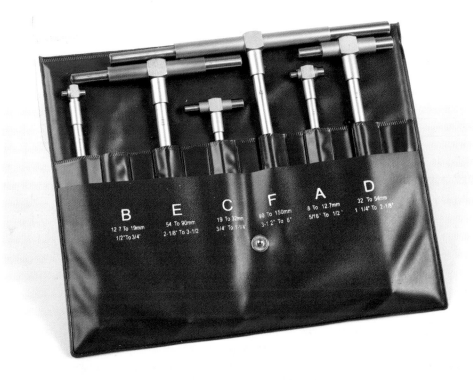

*A set of telescopic gauges for checking a bore, used in conjunction with a micrometer.*

*Boring a hole ready for reaming.*

To bore the hole, the first option is to hold a boring bar in the three-jaw chuck. This is a good basic method of boring a workpiece on the cross slide. The only awkward bit is adjusting the boring bar so that a size hole is bored. This is usually done by an adjusting screw pressing onto the back of the tip opposite the cutting edge. The tip itself is usually clamped by a grub screw through the side of the boring bar. However, you can use a boring bar that is a few thou under the required size and finish off with a reamer.

A similar way that is easier to adjust is to use the same boring bar in the independent four-jaw chuck. Then, instead of adjusting the tip in the boring bar, you can adjust the entire boring bar in the four-jaw chuck. This, as you can imagine, will be a lot easier than trying to adjust the tip in the boring bar.

The third method of boring work on the cross slide is to use a proper boring head. This is easy to adjust as it is designed for this very purpose.

Finally, you could use a 'between centres' boring bar, which is held between the headstock and tailstock centres. This is the only option when you are doing a long bore such as a large cylinder casting for a locomotive or traction engine.

*Boring the hole using the four-jaw chuck method.*

*Using the boring head in the lathe mandrel.*

Unlike when you are facing and boring a component in a chuck, you will not be able to face across the front of the com-

*A flycutter suitable for facing the front of a component that has previously been bored on the cross slide.*

ponent. (Boring heads with the ability to face across the work are available but are unlikely to be found in the amateur's workshop.) This means you will have to face across the work with a flycutter in order to keep the face true with the bore. Flycutters are available quite cheaply or you could make your own and hold it in the four-jaw chuck.

# 11   Knurling, Radius Turning and Production Methods

This chapter explains how to use knurling tools and radius turning tools as well as using basic production methods.

## KNURLING

Knurling is the process of forming or impressing a pattern on a piece of metal, often for the purpose of making a grip for a piece of equipment, such as a knob. Both straight and diamond knurls can be produced, depending on the type of knurl you are using. Diamond knurling is usually done with two knurling wheels, although single-wheel diamond knurls are available.

Knurls are also available in fine, medium and coarse sizes, although the size is relative from different makers. The speed for knurling is usually about half of the turning speed for the same diameter bar. Normal knurling is of the male pattern where the knurling consists of raised pyramids. Female knurling is much rarer and consists of depressed pyramids.

There are three main types of knurling tool but only two of these are found in the average workshop. The first type of knurling tool is the so-called 'cut' knurling tool, which actually cuts a knurl rather than presses the knurl into the work. This is a specialized tool more often used in industry and is very expensive, so it is not found in many home workshops.

### 'Bump' Knurling

The most common knurl is the single- or double-wheel knurl, sometimes called a 'bump' knurling tool. The wheels are mounted at the front of the tool. This type of knurl is pressed into the work by using the cross slide and can produce a good quality knurl. However, it does put very heavy pressure on the mandrel and lathe bearings.

### Straddle Knurling

The best type of knurl for occasional use is the straddle knurl, which has two knurling

*A commercially available straddle knurling tool.*

wheels that completely straddle the workpiece. This type of knurl does not put a strain on the lathe bearings and so is preferred by most lathe users. (Two-wheel knurling tools are available that resemble straddle knurling tools but they don't open up to take anything more than small diameters, relying on pressure at the side of the job like a 'bump' knurl.)

To set the straddle knurl up, wind the tool against a bit of plate held onto the side of the bar. Remove the plate and move the tool in by the thickness of the plate, half the knurl diameter and half the bar diameter. This will put the tool onto the centre line of the bar.

In use, set the knurling wheels to the centre as described above, wind the knurls onto the outside diameter of the bar, wind the knurl away from the bar and move the knurling wheels closer together by twice the depth of the knurl pattern. Switch the lathe on and wind the tool back onto the centre line and the tool should start to form

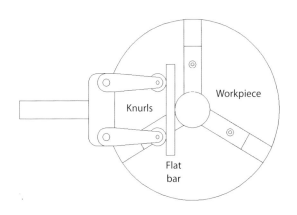

*Setting the knurling tool.*

the knurl. You can now traverse the knurling tool along the workpiece to form the knurl; remember to use cutting oil. Note that the knurls should have chamfered sides if you are traversing along the workpiece.

You need to go deep enough so the knurl is fully formed but not so deep as to deform the knurl. Because the knurl straddles the work, the knurls start off independently and may not be in alignment around the diameter. Once you start moving the knurling tool backwards and forwards along the work, however, the tool should line itself up. This means you may have to turn down, or part off, the bar where you started the knurl.

If you go too deep, especially in aluminium, the whole depth of knurl could get destroyed and even drop off the parent bar. This is called flaking. Knurling is not a difficult process: a little practice will soon have you knurling like a professional engineer.

## RADIUS TURNING

Sometimes we need to form an external radius on the end of a bit of bar, perhaps for

*A form tool cutting a ball. The inset view shows the form tool and a finished ball.*

a ball-shaped handle. We can use a simple lathe attachment to do this. Basically the attachment consists of a short turning tool mounted onto a U-shaped component that is arranged to pivot on another U-shaped component held in the lathe tool post.

By pivoting the attachment back and forth, a radius will be generated. For a true radius the pivot point should be set on the centreline of the bar. The radius generated will depend on how far the tool bit is set back from the centreline of the workpiece.

To set the tool up, wind the attachment up to a plate held to the side of the bar you are working on, remove the plate and wind in the width of the plate, half the width of the bar and the width of the fixture to the centreline of the pin. This will put the pivot on the centre line. Then you can set the tool to the outside diameter of the bar. This will produce a ball the same diameter as the bar.

To turn an internal diameter, use the same method but the turning tool will need to pass through the centre of the pivot and

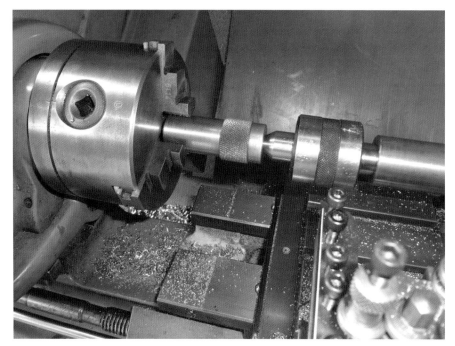

*An accomplished bit of knurling.*

out the other side. You will be limited to shallow depressions rather than large semi-circles but this technique can still be useful on occasion.

The alternative method of forming a ball is with a ball form tool.

## PRODUCTION METHODS

For ease of production, the first thing you need to use is a bed stop (see Chapter 5). The chances are that you will need to make your own. The one I use is very versatile and consists of a block mounted at the front of the lathe headstock, together with a rod to act as the stop.

Depending upon what you are doing, it may be useful to have more than one stop bar, each with its own separate stop block. In use, the bar is inserted into the main block as far as the stop block (if fitted) and locked in place. The first stop bar could be used to face the workpiece and the second (shorter bar) could be used to turn along the diameter, while a third bar could position the parting off tool. An alternative addition to the stop bar could be a washer (or washers) of known thickness; placing the washer (or washers) on the bar will extend the stop position by the thickness of the washers used.

A useful tip is to stamp a number on the stop blocks so that each one is numbered. You could also stamp the thickness on the washers so you don't have to keep measuring them and just pick them up in the correct order. It saves a little time and helps avoid errors.

The whole point about using a stop is the consistency of position, which is transferred to the accuracy of the component it gives. Once you have learnt to use a stop, you will wonder how you managed without it. Even for one-off components it will save you time.

For a typical one-off stepped shaft, set the stop so the turning tool just faces the bar and face off.

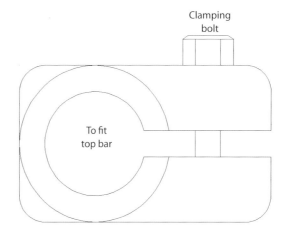

*A stop bar block for the carriage stop.*

Clamping bolt

To fit top bar

Move the top slide along for the length of the turned step required. Turn the step. You now have a step on the end of the bar of a known length. No fiddling, no measuring – you know it is correct.

Using the bed stop offers a simple way of doing repeat turning of lengths and diameters in the lathe. Stops are not limited to production methods; they are very useful for machining one-offs as well.

A single stop bar will serve for much of the work you are doing, but sometimes you need more than one stop. The answer here is to use more than one stop bar in conjunction with a stop block. Each bar has its own stop block that can be tightened up. Then you can interchange the stop bars and each bar can be set to the required length by using a vernier or rule. You just set the two stop blocks to the difference required and lock the stop bar in the holder as normal.

When you need more than one of each item it is very easy to save time in the workshop: once the lathe is set up, you can make several items in quick succession. A typical example of this type of production is a simple spacer. Set a facing and chamfering tool in one tool holder, a parting off tool in another tool holder and a drill in the tailstock chuck. The facing tool and parting off tool are in fixed positions to each other

so it is a simple matter of drilling the hole, facing off with one tool and parting off with the other. As long as the gap between the parting off tool and the facing tool remains constant the spacers will remain at the same width each time you machine one of them.

The easy way to set the thickness of the washer is to face off the end of the bar, bring the parting off tool up to the finished face and lock the cross slide. Wind the parting off tool back slightly so you can move the bar forward in the chuck. Measuring with the vernier calliper's depth rod from the right-hand face of the parting off tool, bring the bar out slightly longer than is needed for the washer thickness. Using the tailstock chuck, drill the hole using a centre drill for the first washer to ensure the drill runs true. Now set the facing tool in position, face off the washer and part off from the bar. Measure the washer and adjust the facing tool either way so that the thickness of the washer is correct. Pull the bar from the chuck slightly further than the facing tool so that each washer can be faced to length. You can make as many washers as you need, all of the same thickness. The same applies to nuts and any other component that needs to be a set length.

If making bolts or screws, the principle is the same but you will need to turn down the diameter to be threaded. This time the difference between the parting off tool and the turning tool is the thickness of the head. In order to face to length, however, a washer of a known size must be inserted between the stop block and the cross slide. This washer will be the length of the turned down portion of the component.

If you want to make a batch of components but don't want to keep moving or changing tools, you can machine the batch one step at a time doing one operation on each component before doing the next operation on all the components. Repeat this until the complete batch ends up as completed components. You have the added advantage that the components will probably all be the same shape and size, something that is not always possible when machining each component individually.

To make a batch of components, such as washers, to the same thickness is quite simple. Set up a parting tool to part off the components and set up a facing tool to face the components. The difference in position between the facing tool and the parting tool will be the thickness of the washers. You can adjust the thickness of the washer by moving the facing tool backwards or forwards with the top slide to adjust it. The rear

parting off tool does not move other than to part off the washer.

## TAILSTOCK TURRET

Another useful accessory is the tailstock turret. This is a rotating head that is usually set back at an angle. It fits into the tailstock of the lathe and has multiple stations to take different tools: often it will take four, five or six tools. The benefit of this is that it can have a bar end stop, a centre drill, a drill, a

*An indexing turret that fits directly into the tailstock of the lathe.*

countersink, a tap and a die or any combination thereof, all set up ready to use in sequence. The tools normally fit into holes bored into the turret. To avoid tools sticking out too far, it is best to use stub drills inserted into round bars that fit into the turret.

You can either drill and tap the round bars or use Loctite to secure the drill in the round bar. You can also buy round adaptors with a Jacobs chuck taper machined on the end to take chucks. Another method of fitting chucks is to drill and tap the round bar to take chucks with threaded extensions. These chucks can often be retrieved from broken Black & Decker type drills.

Die holders can slide on a piece of round rod in the turret. For smaller diameter threads you can stop the die from rotating using your hand. There is no need to reverse the lathe when threading, just stop it and spin the die off by hand; the same goes for taps. For larger taps and dies you can use a short tommy bar to stop rotation, but make sure that the tommy bar position is closer to the work than the end of any of the drills or the tommy bar will snap the drills if you let go of it, or if the tap or die jams up. You can also make or buy a running centre to fit into the turret to save removing it when you need to use a lathe centre. Only do this with small or light work, not heavy bars or for large cuts. When used in conjunction with a good bed stop system a tailstock turret becomes a very versatile production facility.

The turret can be made more versatile by fitting a lever-feed tailstock attachment or a capstan-style feed attachment to the tailstock turret. Either of these attachments will make the turret very fast in operation.

## SECOND OPERATION WORK

Sometimes it is necessary to do second operation work on a part-machined

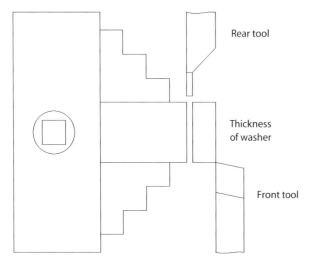

*Making washers to the same length using fixed position tools.*

Rear tool

Thickness of washer

Front tool

*An indexing turret set up with a stop and a centre drill.*

*Standard lever-feed tailstock.*

component. Usually this will be on the opposite end to the one already turned. There are two main ways of holding the workpiece in the correct position for further work: the chuck back stop and soft chuck jaws.

The chuck back stop is quite simple to make. It consists of a draw-in collet, a piece of plain bar for the stop, a bit of threaded bar, a nut and a top hat collar. The collet goes into the lathe mandrel and is drawn in by the threaded bar. The threaded bar goes through the mandrel and is locked in place by the nut and the top hat collar at the left-hand end. The top hat collar is to protect the end of the mandrel. The stop bar fits the collet and is positioned so that the work is located at the right depth in the chuck. This means that each component put into the chuck up against the back stop will always be held in the same position.

*Capstan-style lever-feed tailstock.*

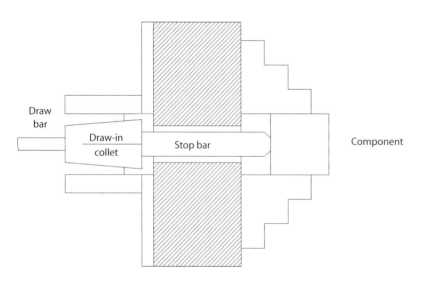

*A draw-in back stop.*

Draw bar

Draw-in collet

Stop bar

Component

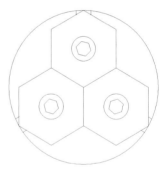

*Soft jaws with hexagons added.*

The second method is to hold the component in soft jaws, which are bored out to hold the component (see Chapter 5). This means the component should run dead true and each one will be held in the same position ready to be machined.

Soft jaws tend to be used for larger components while the back stop is more likely to be used for bar work. You can bolt extension pieces to soft jaws to hold larger diameters or extensions can be machined to make a nest to take larger components. When soft jaws are worn out and faced down too low for further use, you can bolt a piece of hexagon bar to each jaw to give them a new lease of life.

If you have a batch of threaded components to finish on the second end, you can screw them into a bit of bar held in the chuck. If they are hexagon bolts, just tighten up lightly with a spanner; if they are round head, and the head will be machined later, you could tighten and untighten them with a pair of pliers.

The more production work you do, the more varied the methods you will learn, and the quicker you will make components to a high standard of accuracy.

A sensitive drilling attachment can be very useful when drilling with tiny drills. The feed is by hand, which gives it its sensitivity. The attachment can also be used for small taps where the travel is fairly short.

*Machining screw heads by holding the screw in a threaded mandrel.*

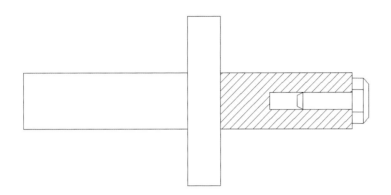

*A sensitive drilling attachment that fits into the tailstock chuck.*

*This Vee attachment is used for cross drilling and can be used in the headstock or the tailstock of the lathe, depending on the length of the bar to be cross drilled.*

*This is a revolving taper for the tailstock. If you fit a drill chuck to it, you can use it as a running support for small bar where a centre is not permissible.*

# *12   Taps, Dies and Screwcutting*

This chapter shows how to use taps and dies to cut internal and external threads in the lathe. It also explains how you can set up a simple gear train and cut a screw thread with the help of a screwcutting dial indicator.

## CUTTING THREADS

Thread cutting, either internal or external, is an important part of learning to use a lathe. The purpose of a thread is usually so that you are able to hold parts together, although other uses for threads, such as leadscrews and feed screws for machine tools, are often called for.

Safety has already been covered in depth (see Chapter 2) but a few extra words on safety when thread cutting are called for. When tapping a hole or threading a bar from the tailstock, a tailstock tap or die holder is often used. For the smaller threads, the holders have a knurled body and rotation can be stopped by simply holding the body of the holder in your hand.

*A typical die.*

As long as you keep your hand away from the chuck and any sharp lathe tools on the cross slide you should be fine (if possible remove either the tool holder or the tool itself). Provided there is nothing to catch or squash your hand on, you can hold the knurled tap or die holder in your hand while the lathe is running slowly under power and releasing the holder when the full length of the thread is cut or the pressure becomes too great for you to stop the rotation. (By slowly, I mean in very slow back gear.)

For larger threads, however, a tommy bar will often need to be used to stop the tap or die holder from rotating. When using the tommy bar to prevent rotation, do not under any circumstances use the lathe under power. Instead, switch the machine right off and unplug it, if possible. Turn the tap or die holding the tommy bar with the right hand and stop the chuck from rotating with the left hand.

There are already many published charts providing thread data covering such factors as tapping hole sizes, minimum, maximum and effective diameters, as well as pitches and threads per inch. I will not be providing them here, but wish to point out that tapping size drills can vary with the material being cut. When I am tapping small sizes in

stainless steel, for example, I usually drill the hole 0.004in (0.1mm) larger than the figure stated in the chart. This way I am less likely to break a tap in the hole.

## HSS or Carbon Steel?

Taps and dies are usually made from carbon steel or HSS. HSS taps and dies tend to remain sharp for much longer than carbon steel taps, but carbon steel is usually cheaper. New carbon steel taps and dies will probably be fine for smaller holes and softer materials, but wherever possible HSS should be your first choice. Second-hand taps and dies are sometimes available from tool shops or on eBay, but in my experience they are often blunt and not worth bothering with.

## Lubricants

Whether tapping, threading with a die or screwcutting, it is normally essential to use a lubricant, even on brass. For brass, aluminium and bronze, kerosene (paraffin) or white spirit is generally used and can, with advantage, have a small amount of cutting oil added.

For steel and stainless steel, a modern paste-based tapping compound or cutting oil should be used. This can also be applied to copper; this metal can be sticky but take it easy and all should go well. I also use paste or cutting oil on cast iron. Although most recommendations are to cut cast iron dry, I have found a lubricant to be very helpful.

## Thread Gauges

When following a published design you will probably use the thread sizes as recommended by the designer. If you are making a thread to match an existing thread, however, you need to figure out what the existing thread is. This is easiest to do on an external thread. If you have only the nut, try to find a bolt that will fit it and use that to check the thread. If you can't find a matching bolt, and the hole in the nut is big enough, you could try pressing a bit of plasticine into the internal thread and measuring that.

To measure the external thread, we need to determine three things using a thread pitch gauge: the outside diameter of the thread; the pitch of the thread; and the thread angle. These three checks will probably be sufficient to decide what the thread actually is.

*Screw thread pitch gauge.*

British threads such as British Standard Fine and British Standard Whitworth, and also the Model Engineer thread system, have an angle of 55 degrees.

American threads such as UNF (Unified Fine), UNC (Unified Coarse), UNEF (Unified Extra Fine), ANF (American National Fine), ANC (American National Coarse) are 60 degrees, as is ISO metric. Unusually, the British Standard Cycle thread is also 60 degrees.

The other thread you might come across

is the BA (British Association) thread. This has a thread angle of 47½ degrees and is metric based. The largest BA thread is 0 BA, which has a 6mm diameter with a 1mm pitch. The BA series go down to 22 BA, but in practice you are unlikely to come across anything smaller than about 14 BA.

## TAPS

Tapping is the process of cutting an internal thread with a tap. First, a hole is centre drilled and drilled in the workpiece. I recommend that you give the top of the hole a 90-degree countersink to give a lead-in to the tap and also to stop the tap from throwing up a burr onto the face of the work.

### Types of Tap

The many types of tap can be divided into

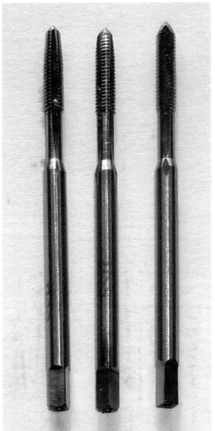

*Set of hand taps.*

hand taps and machine taps. Hand taps are normally held in a tap wrench but can be held in the lathe's tailstock chuck or a purpose-made tailstock tap holder.

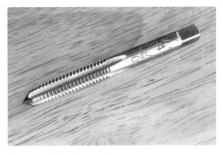

*Close-up of a hand second tap.*

When tapping by hand, start the tap until it starts to bite and give it an extra turn or so. Reverse the direction of the tap for a turn to break the chip. Continue forward for a couple of turns and then reverse as before. Continue to depth, or through the workpiece, by continually tapping a couple of turns, reversing and continuing forward. This should clear the chips and prevent the tap from breaking. If the tap gets hard to turn, take it right out of the hole to clear any swarf, add some more lubricant and continue tapping.

A set of hand taps will normally comprise a taper tap, a second tap and a plug tap. Usually you will start a hole with a taper tap. This is a tap where the outside of the thread is reduced towards the point by grinding it on a taper. This type of tap can be used to start the hole, but if the hole goes right through the work it may be possible to screw the tap right through the hole, so forming a full thread right through.

If the taper tap is too short, or if you are tapping a blind hole, you need to follow the taper tap with the second tap, which has much less of a taper. In fact it only tapers right at the start of the tap.

The plug tap is finally used, usually to finish off a blind hole. The plug tap has no taper on it, just a short lead-in on the end. Between the three, you should be able to tap the majority of holes in the workshop.

When tapping blind holes, it is best to work out the depth and from there the number of turns needed for the tap to reach the bottom of the hole. As an example, say the hole is 9mm deep to the point. The tap enters 2mm into the hole before starting to cut. So, 9mm less 2mm gives 7mm. The pitch of the tap is 0.5 mm; 7mm divided by 0.5 equals 14, so the number of turns to the bottom of the hole is 14. In practice, 12 or 13 turns will be the maximum needed.

When tapping blind holes, make sure that all swarf is removed from the bottom of the hole before starting to tap.

## Holding Taps

There are two main types of tap wrench: the hand tap wrench, which is designed to be held with both hands; and the Tee type tap wrench, which, once started, can often be used one-handed.

Taps usually have either a centre hole drilled in the shank or the shank is ground to a point. This means we can support the tap from the tailstock, either by using a lathe centre or by a bit of bar in the tailstock

chuck with a female centre in it. Tee type tap wrenches often have a female centre in the end and can be supported on a running centre. When the tap is supported by the tailstock at one end and the hole in the workpiece at the other, it must be in line with the hole in the workpiece.

## Machine Taps

The main two types of machine tap are the spiral point and the spiral flute. The spiral point pushes swarf downwards through the hole while the spiral flute pulls the swarf out of the hole. Spiral flute taps are much weaker than spiral point taps and in theory should not be used for tapping by hand. However, in practice you can often get away with hand tapping using a spiral point tap if you are very careful. In either case, the tap is designed for continuous rotation, swarf being automatically cleared, so the regular reversal as with a hand tap is not necessary.

*Machine tap.*

If you are careful you can probably get away with using a hand tap under power, but only do this with a hand-held tap holder where you can quickly let go if the tap starts to stick.

You can also get machine taps that will cut a thread under power by screwing through the job without stopping.

*Spiral flute tap.*

## Speeds for Tapping

Tapping speeds should be low; low back gear speed should be fine. When you have tapped the hole to depth or right through the workpiece, stop the lathe and spin the tap out by hand. This will be quicker than reversing the lathe.

## Threading from the Tailstock

For small taps, you can use the sensitive drilling attachment (see Chapter 11) or, if the tap is larger, you could use a sliding tap holder. This can be as simple as a chuck mounted on a taper at one end with a parallel hole through the chuck shank. The chuck then slides on a bar held in the main tailstock chuck. For large taps you can use a tommy bar to stop the tap holder from turning, but the tommy bar should not be so long as to foul the lathe bed or any other part of the machine if you have to let go. In fact, it is far safer if you do not use the tommy bar to thread under power.

## DIES

Dies also come in carbon steel and HSS versions. The outside diameter of a die often varies with the size of the thread being cut,

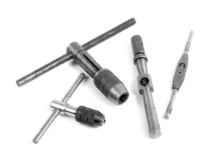

*Selection of tap holders.*

*Sliding tap holder. Sliding die holders are also available.*

although the diameter will be to one of a set standard. Dies usually have the maker's name and the thread details on the front of the die. This is the side that is presented to the work. The die will have a short lead-in; if this is not required on the finished thread you can reverse the die and it will clean up to a shoulder.

When cutting a thread, especially a small one, it pays to make the initial length of thread longer than that required. This is so you have a bit at the front to play with to get the thread right. Then you can part off the excess length leaving a good thread of the required length.

Dies are usually split so you can adjust them to cut a size thread. Ideally you should have a die holder for each die so you can set the die to cut size without having to reset it every time you change the die. The die should be set so that it cuts a size thread in one pass.

Die nuts are often hexagonal in shape. They are used to clean up an existing thread that is damaged, not to cut a new thread from scratch.

For each thread you are going to cut, you should make a home-made gauge tapped with your own tap. When you cut the thread and it fits this gauge, you should then have a good, but not tight or loose, thread.

You should use a tailstock die holder with a sliding body when threading from the tailstock as this will hold the die true to the thread.

Ideally the tailstock die holder should be knurled and also have a tommy bar hole for ease of use.

The speed for threading with a die in the lathe should be quite low; a maximum of 60rpm should be fine for most jobs.

## SCREWCUTTING A THREAD

While cutting a thread with taps and dies is perfectly adequate for most applications, the ability to cut an accurate screw thread by using the lathe is a very useful facility to have. If the thread is large or non-standard, taps and dies may not be available or they may be so expensive as to be out of the question for use in the amateur's workshop.

Various pitches of thread can be cut by the simple expedient of changing the configuration of the change gears or altering the levers on the screwcutting gearbox, if one is fitted. We will concentrate on a lathe with change gears; if you have a screwcutting gearbox, please refer to the manufacturer's handbook.

Most lathes that you will come across are likely to have an imperial pitch leadscrew.

This will be a pitch of so many teeth per inch (TPI). Typically this will be 4 or 8 TPI although other pitches are available. For our example, we will be using a lathe with an 8 TPI leadscrew and a set of changewheels comprising the following numbers of teeth: 2 × 20, 25, 30, 35, 38, 40, 45, 50, 55, 60, 65, 70 and 75.

### Setting Up the Change Gears

Let's take a typical thread pitch of 20 TPI. For every turn of the mandrel the leadscrew needs to move forward 1/20in. This means we have to set the change gears so the mandrel to leadscrew turn ratio is correct. In practice, the mandrel gear is likely to be 20 teeth and this is unlikely to change, no matter what thread we are cutting. This means we will change the leadscrew gear, which has to have the correct ratio to the mandrel.

The TPI we wish to cut is 20, using a leadscrew with a pitch of 8 TPI: 20 divided by 8 gives us a ratio of 2.5:1. This means that the mandrel gear needs to rotate at 2.5 times the leadscrew gear. As the mandrel has 20 teeth, the leadscrew gear needs to be 2.5 times 20 teeth, which is a 50 tooth gear. In practice, a 20 tooth gear and a 50 tooth gear may be too small to transfer the drive from the mandrel to the leadscrew and intermediate gear(s) will need to be used.

These gears are called idler gears and they can have any number of teeth. You may think these idler gears change the ratio of the mandrel to the leadscrew, but they do not. They simply transfer the drive from the mandrel gear to the leadscrew and the ratio stays the same. This concept can be hard to grasp, so I will try to explain it simply.

Say the mandrel gear does one turn. This makes the idler gear or gears move exactly 20 teeth, and this in turn moves the leadscrew gear exactly 20 teeth. As you can see, the ratio does not alter: the leadscrew gear moves 20 teeth for every 20 teeth the mandrel gear moves and the ratio stays the same. This type of set-up is known as a simple gear train.

*Simple gear train.*

*Compound gear train.*

Let us look at another common thread pitch, 32 TPI. The ratio of leadscrew to TPI is 4:1 (8 × 4 = 32). So, the leadscrew gear needs to be the mandrel gear, 20 teeth, times 4 = 80 teeth. Looking at the available gears, we don't have an 80 tooth gear. This means we will have to use a different method to get our 4:1 ratio.

With a mandrel gear of 20 teeth, we could use a 40 tooth to give us a ratio of 2:1. We are now halfway there but need another pair of gears with a 2:1 ratio. We do have a 30 and a 60 tooth gear, so this would give us our second 2:1 ratio. We could not set these gears up as in the previous example, however, since the two intermediate

gears would just act as idlers and the ratio would be 2:1, 50 per cent out from what is required.

What we would have to do is mount the 40 tooth and the 30 tooth gears on the same spindle so they rotate at the same speed as each other. (The 20 tooth gear must drive the 40 tooth gear and the 30 tooth gear must drive the 60 tooth gear in this order.) This would give us the correct 4:1 ratio that we need. As we have mounted two gears on one spindle, this is known as a single compound gear train. Depending on your lathe, you may need an idler gear between the 30 tooth gear and the 60 tooth gear. Again this will not alter the gear ratios.

You can also have double compound gear trains where two lots of gears are mounted together on two spindles. This is taking us into complicated territory, however, and I will refer readers to the screwcutting chart provided for their particular lathe. If your lathe does not come with a screwcutting chart, a search on the Internet should find one that you can download and print out.

The most likely application of double compound gear trains would be to cut metric threads with an imperial leadscrew or imperial threads over 60 TPI.

I have tried to keep this explanation of setting up screwcutting gears simple and the maths to a minimum. The explanation given, together with the screwcutting chart for your lathe, should be more than sufficient to get you going.

## CUTTING THE THREAD

The speed for screwcutting should be about

mid-back gear if you have it, preferably somewhere around 30–40rpm at most.

There are two main methods of screwcutting in the lathe. The first one involves the top slide set parallel to the work and in the other method the top slide is set on an angle to the work.

*External single point screw thread tool setting gauge.*

## Cutting a 20 TPI Thread with the Top Slide Parallel

For a 20 TPI Whitworth thread the pitch is 0.050in and the thread depth is a constant 0.64 of the pitch, so the thread depth is 0.050 × 0.64 = 0.032in. This is the depth the cross slide should be wound in.

While the depth of thread is 0.032in, you also need to move the top slide forward at each pass. For a standard Vee thread this needs to be half the in-feed of the screwcutting tool, so you move the cross slide in by 0.010in and move the top slide along by half this, 0.005in.

*External screw thread tool made from a Coventry die chaser.*

*Cutting a screw thread with the top slide set parallel to the lathe.*

*Cutting a screw thread with the top slide set at an angle to the lathe.*

*The end result, a 20 TPI finished thread, before tidying up the end and undercutting.*

where A is the angle calculated at half the included thread angle minus 1 degree, giving 26.5 degrees; b is the depth of thread (for Whitworth threads, this is 0.64 times the pitch); and c is the calculated angular depth of thread.

For a 20 TPI Whitworth thread the pitch is 0.050in and the thread depth is a constant 0.64 of the pitch, so the thread depth is 0.050 × 0.64 = 0.032in. The compensated depth of thread is then 0.032in divided by the cosine of 26.5 degrees = 0.0357.

## Using the Thread Cutting Indicator

With an 8 TPI leadscrew, if the thread being cut has an even number of threads, the leadscrew can be engaged at any position of the thread cutting dial indicator. If the thread is an odd number, you should use the same number or any alternate number, that is one or three, two or four. For threads with a half pitch, always use the same number. For metric threads or peculiar numbers, do not disengage the clasp nuts, withdraw the screwcutting tool and reverse the motor until the tool goes back to the start. If the thread is an exact multiple of the leadscrew, the clasp nuts can be engaged at any position.

If in doubt, always engage at the same number: one. It takes very little time to traverse the extra distance required.

For leadscrews other than 8 TPI please refer to your lathe manual.

## Cutting a 20 TPI Thread with the Top Slide at an Angle

This angle will vary according to the thread being cut, but it should be about 1 degree less than half the included angle of the thread: for a Whitworth thread of 55 degrees, for example, the angle should be half of 55 degrees minus 1 degree, giving 26.5 degrees. Note that the angle is taken with the top slide set at 90 degrees to the work. With the top slide handle facing you (at 90 degrees to how it is normally used), rotate the top slide the required number of degrees (26.5) to the right. Beginners often rotate the top slide 26.5 degrees to the left from the normal position, which would give an included thread angle of 127 degrees. This is clearly wrong.

Because the top slide is set on an angle, you will need to feed the top slide in further than if the top slide is set parallel to the lathe. You can find the increased depth of thread by using the following formula,

c = b/cosine of A

# Acknowledgements and Useful Contacts

I would like to thank My Time Media Ltd (Publishers of *Model Engineer* and *Model Engineers' Workshop*), Ken Wilson, Tony Jeffree and Transwave, Power Capacitors Ltd for the use of their photographs.

## USEFUL CONTACTS

### United Kingdom

Arc Euro Trade Ltd
10 Archdale Street, Syston, Leicester LE7 1NA
Telephone: 0116 269 5693
Fax: 0116 260 5805
Email: information@arceurotrade.co.uk
http://www. arceurotrade.co.uk
Suppliers of machine tools and accessories

Chester Machine Tools
Hawarden Industrial Park, Hawarden, Chester CH5 3PZ
Telephone: 01244 531631
Email: sales@chestermachinetools.com
http://www.chestermachinetools.com
Suppliers of machine tools and accessories

Cowells Small Machine Tools Ltd
Tendring Road, Little Bentley, Colchester, Essex CO7 8SH
Telephone/Fax: 01206 251 792
Email: sales@cowells.com
http://www.cowells.com
Suppliers of the Cowells range of lathes and milling machines, including a clockmaker's lathe.

Transwave Converters
Power Capacitors Ltd
30 Redfern Road, Tyseley, Birmingham B11 2BH
Telephone: 0800 035 2027
Email: transwave@powercapacitors.co.uk
http://www.transwaveconverters.co.uk
Inverter and converter manufacturers

Warco
Warco House, Fisher Lane, Chiddingfold, Surrey GU8 4TD
Telephone: 01428 682929
Fax: 01428 685870
Email: sales@warco.co.uk
http://www.warco.co.uk
Suppliers of machine tools and accessories

### USA

Grizzly Industrial, Inc.
1821 Valencia Street, Bellingham, Washington 98229
Telephone: 1-800-523-4777
http://www.grizzly.com
Suppliers of machine tools and accessories

Harbor Freight
3491 Mission Oaks Boulevard, PO Box 6010, Camarillo, California 93011-6010
Telephone: 1-805-444-3353
http://www.harborfreight.com
Suppliers of machine tools and accessories

### Australia

Carba-Tec Pty Ltd
128 Ingleston Road, Wakerley, Queensland 4154
Telephone: (07) 3390 5888
Fax: (07) 3890 5280
Email: orders@carbatec.com.au
http://www.carbatec.com.au
Suppliers of machine tools and accessories

Hare & Forbes Machineryhouse
'The Junction', Unit 1, 2 Windsor Road, Northmead, New South Wales 2152
PO Box 3844, Parramatta, New South Wales 2124
Telephone: (02) 9890 9111
Fax: (02) 9890 4888
http://www.machineryhouse.com.au/Stores
Suppliers of machine tools and accessories

### New Zealand

Carba-Tec NZ Pty Ltd
110 Harris Road, East Tamaki, Auckland
Telephone: 09 274 9454
Fax: 09 274 9455
Email: orders@carbatec.co.nz
Suppliers of machine tools and accessories

# *Index*

# Related Titles from Crowood

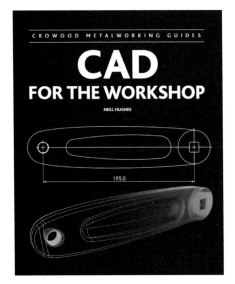

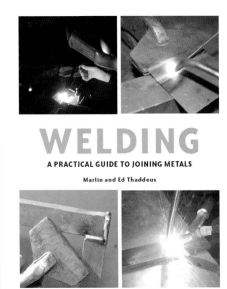

*For further information about these and other Crowood publications,*
*visit our website www.crowood.com.*